The Secret Self of Socialism

From Owen to Orwell

"Pig Bother is watching you!"

The Secret Self of Socialism

From Owen to Orwell

Denise Carrington-Smith

Storixus

First published 2022 by
Storixus Independent Publishing
Canberra, Australia

www.storixus.com

ISBN 978-0-6454958-2-9 (Paperback Edition)
ISBN 978-0-6454958-3-6 (eBook Edition)

For the first time he perceived that if you want to keep a secret you must also hide it from yourself.

– George Orwell

1984. Part 3, Chapter 4.

Content

Introduction

We are a strange species, us humans. So many different faces, so many different 'persona'. There is the 'face' we show only to our closest partner, another to our friends. The 'face' we show to our children when they are little is different from the one they see when they are older. Then they see the 'face' of a friend – or, possibly, an acquaintance, if circumstances create distance. The 'face' we show at the workplace is different again, as is the one seen by the boss, the one seen by our work-mates and that seen by our customers. Then there are the 'faces' displayed during leisure activities – the serious student at art class, the care-free one at line-dancing. That which is our 'true' self is known only to us.

Or is it?

It is said that each of us has a secret self, one so secret that even we do not know it. We may like to think we know ourselves, how we will react under different circumstances. We might like to think that we would dash fearlessly into a burning building to save our child, or even our pet dog or cat. But would we? Until the circumstance arises, none of us will ever know. Happily, most of us will die without ever knowing. Perhaps, one day, you may surprise yourself by 'rising to the occasion'. We have all seen people being interviewed on television after having performed some act of bravery or endurance. Often they look quite bemused. "I just did what anyone would do." "I don't know what came over me. I just jumped in and grabbed him." Sometimes it is as though a different force has taken over our being – and not always for the better. The 'something came over me' explanation is often cited by those who have done something horrendous, especially murder.

We, as individuals, may not know ourselves as well as we think we do. May this also be true of groups of people? Is it possible that groups of people may have a 'secret self' which propels them in a direction not foreseen or intended?

Do businesses have a secret self? Do religions have a secret self? Do political parties? Does socialism have a secret self? Has it been led along a path completely unforeseen by its founder, even though he was the one who led the way?

In England, that person is often claimed to have been Robert Owen, although that may not be strictly true. If Socialism is rule by the people, or their representative, rather than by an hereditary monarch, then the founder of Socialism in Britain was Oliver Cromwell, who led the rebellion of 1649 which resulted in the overthrow of Charles I. There was little bloodshed at the time. Only one person died – the King, who was beheaded. The bloodshed came afterwards. England's monarchs had always been, more or less, democratic. Their right to rule was confirmed by the people at the coronation. Charles I had made the mistake of copying the French kings, claiming a 'Divine Right to Rule'. Cromwell may have presented himself to the people as their liberator, but he quickly became their dictator. The fact that his son, briefly, followed him as Lord Protector is evidence of how quickly the concept of hereditary succession reasserted itself. There then followed England's only Civil War, won by the 'Loyalist' Royalists. Charles II rode into London on 30th April, 1660, his 30th birthday, to reclaim the throne.

Could Socialism exist under a monarch? Some thought so. Robert Owen thought so. Abraham Lincoln did not. The American Civil Libertarians did not ask for their own Parliament, the right to make their owns laws. They demanded the overthrow of the Monarch. Their new ruler, whom they called 'President', was chosen by the people, the position could not be held for more than eight years, and was not hereditary, a system which has lasted for more than 250 years.

Then came France. The bloodshed which accompanied – and followed – the French Revolution shocked the world. Once again, the man who offered to overthrow the despot became one himself. Accepting the title of 'Emperor', Napoleon set out to rule over all of Europe and part of Asia, with his incursion into Egypt. The British put paid to that one, but once again, it was the Emperor's son who took over rulership. This pattern has been repeated again and again: the charismatic person holding out the hope of liberation from a dictatorial monarch has become a dictator himself: Franco, Mussolini, Hitler, Stalin, Chairman Mao, Jomo Kenyatta, Idi Amin, Robert Mugabwe, Peron, Pinochet, Pol Pot, Kmher Rouge, the list goes on and on. What is happening here? Were these people ever truly 'Socialists'. Did they think they were? What is 'Socialism' anyway?

Time to take a look at its foundations, its founder, Robert Owen – and the socialist philosophers who followed him.

1

The Launch of Robert Owen

I had become (vaguely) familiar with the name of Richard Owen during my study of archæology. He was one of the early experts in the study of dinosaurs. Animal fossils are only of interest to archæologists in connection with past human development and activity, which, alas, excluded dinosaurs, so the name 'Owen' remained obscure in my mind. It was enough, however, to pique my interest when it came up a few times during my study of the life and work of Alfred Russel Wallace, who, I believe, expounded the theory of evolution by natural selection before Charles Darwin (Carrington-Smith 2022). There was only one problem. Wallace was not referring to Richard Owen, but Robert. Who was this 'Robert', who had been so influential in Wallace's younger days? I needed another project. Robert Owen was as good as any.

I could not help but smile when I started to read Podmore's two volume biography of Robert Owen, published in 1906. Frank Podmore (1856-1910) had embarked upon this undertaking for much the same reason as had I: he needed a project and the subject seemed interesting. He wrote 'for pleasure'. In his *Preface*, Podmore told how, as his work progressed, he became more and more aware of its importance and wondered whether some 'other force' had inspired him, guided him, in the undertaking of his task. Socialism was on the rise and many people described Robert Owen as the 'Father of Socialism'.

Little did Podmore imagine what was to come! The fall of the German Royal Family as the result of the Great War; the fall of the Tsar with the Russian Revolution, the Red Revolution in China, the Second World War, the break up of the British Empire, increasing colonial independence, with the consequent establishment of many Socialist (Democratic) Republics, especially in Africa and South America.

Podmore discovered that, towards the end of his life, Owen had started to write his own *Autobiography*. Only the first volume was completed, covering the first fifty years of his life (until 1820), being published in 1857 when Owen was 86 years old, The book was long out of print and difficult to obtain. Podmore saw no point in rewriting that which Owen had already written. He made the very sensible decision merely to reproduce Volume 1, with additions in square brackets [ ]. The second volume was the result of Podmore's extensive research. In addition to Owen's autobiography, four biographies of Owen had been written in 1860, 1866, 1869 and 1886. A collection of letters, written both to and from Owen, had been found, he believed in 1903 – just as he was starting his writing, Of these he made much use. If you want to know more about Owen than is contained herein, then Podmore's two volume work is a good place to start. I also accessed *Life of Robert Owen* by Frederick Adolphus Packard (1866), which was valuable because he wrote with the intention of pointing out the flaws in Owen's thinking, being staunchly anti-socialist. With all of this, there was a problem. Referencing!

Owen thought, experimented with his ideas, and, after twenty-five years of practice, finally considered he was justified in presenting his ideas to the world in 1816. He started lecturing, writing articles, writing books, travelling within the British Isles, Europe and America. While he honed his ideas, extrapolated upon them, he never changed them. The result was constant repetition, sometimes almost word for word. Later writers reproduced some of his work: a sentence, a paragraph, a section, a complete article, extracts from complete books. This made referencing very difficult. In addition to the standard *References* at the end of this book, l have included a *Bibliography* at the end of chapter 5, which includes all the 'Owen' books l read. Good luck!

Robert Owen was born on 14th May, 1771, in the village of Newtown, Montgomeryshire, in the north of Wales, the sixth of seven children. Two of his siblings died young; William, Anne and John were older than he, Richard younger. He claimed that by the time he was seven years old, he could read and write fluently. He further claimed that he was reading 'a book a day'. He read both fact and fiction for about five hours a day. Around the age of eight or nine, he became an 'usher' at school, the term being given to an older child who helped the teacher instruct the younger pupils.

At that time, Newtown was a small country town of about one thousand inhabitants. His father, also named Robert, had been born in Welsh Pool and was saddler, ironmonger, post master and had general management of parish affairs. He married into the Williams family, among the most respectable of farming families in the area. His mother was the eldest daughter of the family. This last piece of information took my attention. Although l lived in London for most of the war, for the final year (April 1944-April 1945) l was evacuated to North Wales, where l became a student in a small primary school for girls, about forty students, which had been relocated to a Manor House just outside Newtown as part of the Government evacuation programme. The owner of the Manor House was Mr. Williams! Must be the same family, surely? There couldn't be two Williams families with large properties just outside Newtown, could there? Did l spend a year of my life sheltering beneath the same roof which had sheltered Owen's mother in her childhood?

Bored at school, the young Robert earned pocket money 'after hours' helping a neighbour with haberdashery, drapery and also some grocery business, first on market days, then every day. He does seem to have been a responsible youngster. He records that he was never 'but once' corrected by his parents. That 'once' is worth noting. His mother asked him something. He misunderstood and answered 'No'. His mother asked him again. He realised his mistake, but refused to admit it, continuing with his refusal, although it resulted in a beating, the only one he ever had. The refusal to admit to being wrong was a hallmark of Owen's character. On this occasion, he admitted to his reader that he had been in the wrong – the only time he ever did so. For the rest of his life, he thought things over carefully, came to a conclusion, and stuck with it, come hell or high water!

Owen recorded three significant events from his childhood. One morning, he started to eat his breakfast of 'flummery' (a form of porridge) when it was too hot. His throat was scalded. He fell unconscious and remained so for such an extended period of time that his parents thought he was dead. From that time onward, he could only eat small quantities of simple foods. "I have always thought that this accident had a great influence in forming my character" (Podmore 1906: 6). I believe so, too. Being qualified both as a psychologist and a natural therapist, many people consulted me about 'mental' problems, such as change of character. Something would come over these people and they would act in a manner not in accordance with their usual personality. Some people described it as a profound mood change; others averred that another 'personality' took over their body: they were temporarily 'displaced'. Many could name their alternate 'personality' – or 'personalities', often there was more than one. This condition is generally referred to as 'dual personality', 'split personality' or 'multiple personality' disorder. I learned to expect a history of some 'near death' experience, drowning, high fever from which recovery had not been expected, and so on. It was as if the aura had been damaged and another entity had been enabled to penetrate, sometimes briefly, intermittently, sometimes for longer periods, occasionally permanently. Happily, some of the remedies at my disposal seemed to be able to heal the energy field surrounding the body, as well as the body itself, and these episodes ceased. Such people 'network'. I found myself dealing with more and more of these people. Occasionally, one came across a person, like Owen, who seemed to have benefited from the experience, feeling themselves to be 'overshadowed' by some higher force. It matters not whether I believe it, or whether you believe it. What matters is that Owen believed it! He was convinced that he was on a mission and that that mission had been ordained, and was supported, by a higher force. Success was inevitable – eventually!

Owen recounted two other experiences. Once his finger had become stuck in a keyhole. He twisted his finger so painfully attempting to remove it that he was found, unconscious, on the floor, but his finger had been released. Another time, he tried to cross a bridge on horseback when a carriage was coming in the other direction. His leg was in danger of being crushed by the wheel of the carriage so he flung it across the saddle, putting himself in danger of being crushed against the wall or flung over the bridge. He awoke to find himself lying on the footpath of the bridge, his horse standing quietly beside him, the carriage passing into the distance. Thus ended his account of his childhood escapades, but not of his childhood.

Owen described himself as being deeply religious. He particularly emphasised his early interest in books on religion – not just on Christianity but Judaism, Hinduism, the religions of the Mahomedans, the Chinese and the Pagan. He had access to many books, the libraries of the local clergyman, physician and lawyer being made open to him. He could borrow any book he wanted. He mentioned several books he had read, among which I recognised *Robinson Crusoe, Pilgrim's Progress* and *Paradise Lost*. He also read books on travel, such as that written by the early 'Travel Agent', Thomas Cook, and "all the circum-navigators' voyages" (Silver 1969: 42). It was in this context that he made his claim to have read a book a day.

The young Robert was particularly troubled by what he came to see as religious hypocrisy. If the ten Commandments had been ordained by God, they should be obeyed, yet many people blatantly disregarded instructions in regard to the teachings regarding the Sabbath. At around age twelve, he wrote to the Prime Minister, Mr. Pitt, "expressing the hope that Government would adopt some measure to enforce better observation of the Sabbath". A Government proclamation a few days later enjoined stricter observance (Podmore 1906: 21-22).

Owen remembered going out early in the morning to walk in the park – and think. This he did for three or four hours, in summer, weather permitting, and again in the evening. Presumably the reading was done mostly in the winter months? All adherents of a particular religion claimed to be right, to believe in the one true religion. They could not all be right – but they could all be wrong! By the age of ten, Robert had come to the conclusion that all religions had emanated from the same source, an acknowledgement of the existence of some unknown Creative Force. It was all the added bits which were the problem.

He came to another, and in some ways more important, conclusion (Silver 1969: 44):

> My reason taught me that I could not have made one of my own qualities – that they were forced upon me by Nature – that my language, religion, and habits, were forced upon me by society, and that I was entirely the child of Nature and Society; - that Nature gave the qualities and Society directed them.

People were brought up in a certain religion, or sect of a religion, as dictated by the society, or the position within society into which they had been placed, usually at birth. Why should any person receive praise or blame for that? Furthermore, and this in some ways was an even greater insight, people had no control over the strata of society into which they were born – prince or pauper. Some people received a 'good' upbringing, others did not. Some people behaved well, as adults, others did not, even ending up in prison. How sure could the more privileged people be that, had they been born under different circumstances, they, too, would not have ended up in prison?

All souls were equal. All should be treated the same.

Both the American and French Revolutions had promised equality, following the violent overthrow of the aristocratic class. Had their promise been fulfilled? No, was the simple answer. France now had an Emperor and America its rich, who were becoming richer, an upper echelon, without titles maybe, but as aristocratic in their outlook as any person in Europe.

Things needed to change and Owen devoted his life to bringing that change about.

2

Manufacturing Happiness

Robert Owen left school at the age of ten, nothing particularly unusual about that for the time in which he was living. What was more unusual was that he left home at the same age, ten, moving to London. Why London? Why so far away? The answer to that is quite simple – his older brother, William, then in his twenties, was living in London and Robert went to live with him.

The arrangement did not last long. His brother, having finished his apprenticeship, married the owner (who was a widow) and took over the business, which was a sizeable clothing store. It would seem that William had contacts with manufacturers in the clothing industry because six weeks later he obtained an apprenticeship for Robert with a Mr. McGuffog in Stamford, Lincolnshire. The McGuffogs owned a large store, trading the finest quality fabrics. As an apprentice, Robert became one of the family, living with them, his board and lodging being the greater part of his remuneration. The first year of his apprenticeship, he received no further pay; the second year he was paid 'forty dollars', the third 'fifty'. I use inverted commas for these amounts, because Packard, being American, gave the sums in dollars, not pounds.

Owen attended Church with the McGuffogs on Sunday – twice. Mr. McGuffog was Scottish Presbyterian, Mrs. McGuffog English Episcopalian, so both attended both churches. Two

Christian Churches, two somewhat different beliefs, each claiming they were right, the other in error, although Owen did state that he never heard a word of argument between husband and wife. The situation offended Robert's logical mind, as did the concept that heaven or hell, reward or punishment, awaited the soul after death for believing what it had been taught to believe. It was during this time that he wrote to Mr. Pitt regarding the Sabbath. It was also during this time that he abandoned belief, not only in the doctrines taught by the two Churches he attended, but in Christianity itself, finding an incredible sense of relief. All feelings of guilt had been lifted away. He condemned no one for their belief; he condemned no one for their actions, because he had come to the conclusion that actions resulted from character, for which the individual was not responsible.

While Joseph Locke postulated that each child was born a *tabula rasa*, an empty slate, his was a minority opinion. Most people accepted that each child, from birth, was possessed of a distinct individual character, which character remained throughout life, moderated, perhaps, but never completely changed. From whence had this character been obtained. From God? From one's ancestors (DNA in today's parlance)? From God, said Owen, and most people agreed with him since there were few atheists in those days. No one questioned that {human) society asserted a great influence. Indeed, the Church deemed it necessary for a child, not only to have two parents to care for their physical needs, but three 'Godparents' (two of the same sex as the child and one of the opposite) who would be responsible for the child's spiritual development, which task was deemed to be the more important.

You will have noticed that Owen omitted the third influence, postulated not only by the Abrahamic religions, but accepted by every other religion and society of which I am aware – free will, or, as the Bible put it, the knowledge of good and evil. (Christian) people at that time believed that animal behaviour was governed by instinct. Humans, alone, were capable of logical thought, had the ability to make their own decisions, for better, for worse. Today, having watched endless hours of 'wildlife' documentaries, as well as candid camera vision of our domestic friends, our cats and dogs, when their owners are out and they believe themselves to be unobserved, we know that this is not true. We have witnessed lion cubs, baby chimps, young meercats, all testing the boundaries of what is acceptable and paying the price with a paw around the ear, or a bite on the shoulder, if they make the wrong decision! Horses and dogs can be trained because they have the ability to distinguish right from wrong, to learn new patterns of behaviour. Cats, too, have very distinct ideas of right and wrong – they are right, you are wrong! However, even if Owen had acknowledged these facts, it would have made no difference to his theory. He would have assumed that animals were born with certain individual characteristics, as were humans, and then shaped by their society, as were humans,

Owen had one characteristic which was most praiseworthy. Patience! In his early youth, he read, he observed, he thought, and he came to certain conclusions, but he kept his thoughts to himself. As he set out into the world, he continued to think and observe. Very gradually, opportunity came for him to put some of his ideas into practice, but it was not until some twenty years later that he made them public. For around a further twenty years, he shared his ideas by inviting people of influence, and other interested people, to visit his manufactory, which they did, not merely by the hundreds, but by the thousands. It was not until he reached retirement age that he ended his personal involvement with his business, spending the remainder of his life travelling to promote his ideas, within Britain, Ireland, Europe and America. Even this was in keeping with his notion of the ideal life plan, as will become clear.

All souls were equal in the sight of God. All people should be equal in the sight of humans. All were equally entitled to a share in the wealth of the nation. No person, or group of people, should be privileged. If one person was more gifted than another, for example, better at art or music, more athletic, displayed more business acumen, then that was not something of which to be proud, because that person had done nothing to deserve their good fortune. If anything, it was a burden because it placed upon them the duty to share their gift, where possible, with others less fortunate. And if someone was lazy, made little effort? That was not their fault; if the Divine had not blessed them with energy, enthusiasm, ambition, they could not be blamed. Each person should be encouraged to do their best, which, after all, is all that anybody can do. Later this was to be expressed by Karl Marx as "From each according to his ability; to each according to his need". It didn't work then, either.

By the time Owen left home to start his adult, working, life, he had already come to the basic beliefs which were to stay with him the rest of his life. It was these beliefs which guided his business practices from the very start. He did not acquire his beliefs as the result of his businesses; he developed his businesses in accordance with his beliefs.

After completing his apprenticeship, Robert left the McGuffogs. paying a brief visit to his parents in Newtown, before taking up a position with Messrs. Flint and Palmer, an established business on old London Bridge, overlooking the River Thames. He received a salary of €25 per annum, describing himself as feeling "rich and independent" (Podmore 1906: 21). There was clearly a difference between the value of the pound and the dollar. Working at this apartment store was quite a shock to the system. Starting work at 8 a.m. might not sound too much of an imposition, but he needed to be correctly dressed first. He had to wait his turn with the hairdresser, for his hair to be powdered and curled, one curl down each side of his face and a stiff pig-tail at the back! Staff were expected to be as well-dressed as any customer. The apartment store remained open until ten, or ten-thirty at night, after which the shop needed to be tidied, ready for the next day, with all the jumbled up/turned over wares neatly replaced in their correct position. It was often 2 a.m. before they were free to stagger up to bed, with the aid of the banister. Meals were taken in between customers, when a few mouthfuls could be snatched. After the spring trade, things did improve and he might be in bed by eleven or twelve at night. Meals became more reasonable. Owen described himself as having been 'kindly treated' and was almost sorry when a friend, as the result of an earlier request, announced that he had found him an alternative position with a Mr. Satterfield in Manchester. Pay was €40 a year. This was 1787. He turned eighteen, becoming a man, his boyhood being behind him.

It was while he was working at Satterfield's that he came into contact with visiting salesmen. One of these salesmen was a Mr. Jones, who told Owen of new machinery for the spinning of cotton. If only he could raise €500 capital, he could start his own business. If Owen could come up with the money, Owen could have a half share of the profits – so Owen did! That is not strictly true. It was Owen's brother, William, who came up with the capital, Owen who took a share of the profits. He earned them. Jones, apparently, had no business sense. Owen took over all the financial management of the business, which was situated in a large shop, built for the purpose, with forty male employees.

From employee to employer – Owen's transition from boyhood to manhood was complete – and a very successful transition it proved to be. Following Arkwright's lead, others were looking to improve machinery in the burgeoning cotton industry. Jones and Owen made things called 'mules', which had been invented by a man named Crompton, who had failed to patent them, whether from ignorance or magnanimity, who can now say? The mules performed the final stage of manufacture, initial production being on Arkwright's machines, but it was that final stage which made Jones/Owen's threads the finest available.

Another investor approached Jones, interested in taking up a share in the business. Owen was consulted, and consented, but: two's company, three's a crowd! Owen soon asked to be allowed to relinquish his share, not for cash but for six 'mules', a reel and a make up machine. Only three were ever received, but these proved to be enough – and were probably all Owen expected, if his subsequent business behaviour (over valuing and then accepting less) is anything to go by! The business quickly became profitable. He employed three men and in his first year his business turned over a profit of €300. It was 1790 and Owen had not yet turned twenty. Soon he had forty employees and the business was thriving.

Then Owen had a stroke of luck. It appeared to come about due to another person's bad luck, but both parties ended up by benefiting, which is the best type of 'good luck' there is. Another manufacturer, a Mr. Drinkwater, described as 'a wealthy merchant of Manchester' (Packard 1866: 20) had been about to embark upon the improvement and enlargement of his business when his manager deserted him. Owen applied for the position. Mr. Drinkwater was doubtful about Owen's age and experience, but his enthusiasm (and satisfactory references) won the day. Owen had asked (demanded) a salary of €300 a year, which astounded Mr. Drinkwater. They reached a compromise: Owen received the salary requested and Mr. Drinkwater acquired Owen's machinery at cost price. Owen now found himself in charge of five hundred men, women and children.

When Owen entered the factory on the first day, he was overwhelmed by the enormity of the task which he had so recklessly taken over. With a commonsense and maturity beyond his years, Owen set about learning the business – from his employees (Silver 1969: 46):

> I looked grave, - inspected everything very minutely ... I was with the first in the morning, and I locked up the premises at night ... I continued this silent inspection for six weeks, saying merely yes or no to the questions of what was to be done or otherwise and during that period I did not give one direct order about anything."

What patience! What wisdom in a person who had not yet reached the age of majority! His mental rectitude was all the more extraordinary when it is noted that it was coupled with physical agility. Owen tells us that he had been the fastest runner in his class and the best dancer in the school. His love of dancing remained with him throughout his life. So quick in the one area, so cautious in the other!

Gradually, he made changes. The product improved. Indeed, Drinkwater's fabrics were held to be the finest available. The business improved. Mr. Drinkwater was happy. Owen was happy. He particularly mentioned that at this time, already freed from religious prejudice and convinced that no person was responsible for their own character or capabilities, Owen bonded with his workforce on an equal basis. He then came to realise that he actually had a greater degree of influence over their behaviour (order and discipline) than he had ever had before. The people worker harder, were more sober, and, most importantly, were more happy because they were earning more money! Everybody was happy because everybody's interest were being addressed. More people were happy when more people were happy. How hard was that to understand? Quite, apparently, if the current state of affairs throughout the country, and, indeed, the world, was to be believed!

Drinkwater's traded with companies in Scotland. Owen became well-respected and started to make some influential friends, among whom were John Dalton, scientist and philosopher, who was then propounding his novel 'undefined atomic theory' and the philosopher, Samuel Coleridge. He was invited to join Societies, even serve on a committee. He started to mix with persons of other walks of life, for example, medical men and aristocrats. Most people were either merchants, or doctors, or philosophers, or land owners. His wide ranging interests made him welcome in many different environments.

When he mentioned to his friends that he intended to manage his work force by understanding and kindness rather than criticism and punishment, they smiled. He was not deterred. Drinkwater's factory had been the first ever built to accommodate Sir Richard Arkwright's new cotton-spinning machinery. Now Drinkwater's had the mules as well. Little did the workers know that they were innovators on *two* fronts, machinery and management. That Drinkwater appreciated his efforts was shown by his increasing Owen's salary by 'five hundred dollars' in his second year of employment, a similar amount in the third and an offer of partnership in the fourth.

This was when everything went wrong!

Somebody else, a Mr. Oldknow, proposed a partnership, not just between his company and Drinkwater's, but between himself and Drinkwater's daughter! Owen was approached, as a matter of form, with regard to a new (three-sided) partnership, which he refused, destroying his deed, on the spot, resigning his position as manager (Podmore: 47). He received a number of offers of partnership, eventually merging Messrs. Borrowdale and Atkinson of London and Messrs. Barton of Manchester to form the Chorlton Twist Company in 1795. In the course of his duties, Owen visited other manufactories in the north of England and Scotland. While in Glasgow, a mutual friend introduced him to a nineteen-year-old young lady, one Caroline Dale, who invited him to visit the cotton mills at New Lanark, owned by her father, the merchant and philanthropist, David Dale.

3
New Lanark

Owen described himself as reserved, shy, especially in the company of the female sex. There is no indication that, up until that time (his late twenties) he had ever been engaged in any female pursuit and, if he is to be believed (and I see no reason why not) it was not he who now did the pursuing! Be that as it may, Owen was soon to find himself married. Miss Dale had kindly offered to arrange for him to visit her father's mills, which he did. She asked him to call to see her afterwards to tell of his impressions, which he did. She told him that her father was thinking of retiring, of selling. She suggested Owen approach her father with an offer, which he did.

Mr. David Dale was a Scotsman, born in 1738. He had founded the mill in 1784, or, rather, Richard Arkwright had founded it, he had funded it! Dale was a merchant and a banker, a magistrate and a lay-preacher. He was not actively involved with the running of the business, which was, at that time, under the management of his younger half brother, Miss Dale's Uncle James. Arkwright had died in 1792, at the age of 60. I am sure Mr. Dale was more than happy to receive an offer from a person so well known and respected in the cotton business as Robert Owen had by then become, a worthy successor to Mr. Arkwright. Packard (1855: 51) stated that Owen offered three hundred thousand dollars which offer was accepted. According to Podmore (1906: 50), Owen offered €60,000, payable at the rate of €3,000 *per annum* over a period of twenty years. Whichever version you choose to accept, at the age of 27, just as the century turned, Owen became owner of the mills at New Lanark. Of course, he did not have that amount of money himself − nor did his ever helpful brother, William. No. Owen was now in the big league, needing to find investors, which he did.

Earlier I referred to Mr. Dale as a philanthropist. From the time he had started work, he had given part of his wages to the poor. He not only became a lay preacher, he established his own sect: "Old Scotch Independents". He was a pastor for forty years, ministering, not only to his own congregation, but travelling around the country (Scotland) setting up other branches of his Church. He paid for the education of some four hundred children. It was not surprising that he welcomed the young Robert Owen into his family.

As was standard practice at that time, the couple were engaged for two years before they finally married. Owen had been living in "a very expensive mansion, with a walled garden and pleasure grounds attached, near Manchester" (Packard 1855: 53). The property actually belonged to Mr. Dale. Owen lived (alone) in a small part thereof, renting out the remainder and it was here that the couple lived for the first three months of their married life, after which they moved into their own (much smaller) place. It would seem that Owen delegated the day-to-day management of the Mills to trusted employees, which would have been appreciated by them.

Fortunately, Owen was practised in patience! At the New Lanark Mills, he repeated the same cautious approach that he had undertaken so successfully in Manchester. About two thousand persons were resident in New Lanark, of those about five hundred were 'orphanage' children, who worked in the Dale factory. The site had been chosen because of the river and waterfall, which provided water-power. The village consisted of "three or four rows of grey stone houses, and four gaunt cotton-mills, seven storeys high" (Podmore 1906: 81). Dale had been a benevolent, if absent, boss. He employed orphanage children, not just because child labour was cheap, but because he was giving them an opportunity to learn skills which, it was hoped, would serve them well when they left his employ at the end of their five year apprenticeship. The children were fed, housed and clothed as well as any; he offered them some chance to learn the basics of reading and writing by attending instruction after work, but work hours were so long that those that did attend were prone to fall asleep in class.

It is understandable that the local adults, who had also been employed by Dale, were suspicious of their new employer. The chances of him being harder, not more generous, were extremely high. Furthermore, he was a foreigner, came from England, (even if he was Welsh). Any small change proposed by Owen was greeted with suspicion. He gradually earned their trust, but that took years, not weeks or months. Furthermore, Owen might be the manager, but, from a financial prospective, he was the minor partner and he needed to be very aware of his partners' expectation of profit.

You may be surprised to learn that one of the first changes Owen made was to end the agreement with the orphanages for the placement of children. Only those previously agreed were accepted. After that, all employees were families. Owen was intent on building a community and for that he needed permanent residents – residents who would not only be employed at the mills for their entire working lives, but who would be followed by their children, for generations to come. Most mills operated on a twelve hour working day – six days a week. The actual time at the mills varied between thirteen and fourteen hours, depending upon time allowed for meal breaks, which was never less than an hour, mostly one-and-a-half, allowing for two 'snack' breaks. Occasionally hours were longer, up to fifteen. Today, such hours seem almost criminal, so why were they so widely accepted? Was it greed? Was it need? Or was it habit – that was just the way things were?

I believe the last answer to be the correct one. During the mid 1950s, for about a year I had a boyfriend whose family were dairy farmers. Sometimes I stayed at the farm while he enjoyed his rostered weekend off. His father and three brothers arose soon after 4 a.m., enough time for a cuppa and bite to eat before starting work (promptly) at 5 a.m. Cows were fed, milked, washed down and put out to pasture. By 9 a.m., they (the farmers, not the cows) were back for a full English breakfast. By ten o'clock, they were at work again. Stalls had to be cleaned, restocked with fresh fodder. Those huge 'cans' of milk had to be dragged up the ramp into the lorry for delivery to the marketing depot. One o'clock was lunch time – or was that dinner time, seeing it was the main meal of the day? A short rest, another cup of tea, then back at work. Time for the second milking session. The cows knew their way, but it still took the men time to open all the gates. Each cow found its own way home to is own stall, beautifully identified by a handsome, carved plaque bearing her name, hung on the wall above the feeding trough. The plaques were not to remind the farmers of the cow's name – they knew that – but to remind everybody that the stall belonged to the cow. It was *her* home and humans entered with her permission, which they always 'requested' before they entered. Another round of milking. Another round of feeding. Another round of showering – this time of humans - before, at about 7.30 p.m. they gathered around the table for supper – soup, something on toast, tea and biscuits/cake and then, around 9 p.m. - bed! They each enjoyed one day and one afternoon off one week and a weekend off the next – more generous than the one day a week's 'rest' enjoyed by the Mill employees, but otherwise the hours were not so very different.

When, in the eighteenth century, farm employees, whose ancestors had worked similar hours for centuries, millennia, moved from country to town, it did not seems strange for them to work the same hours. But why would a country person voluntarily move from the countryside, exchanging sunshine and fresh air for the enclosed space of the factory? There is a two-word answer to that question: Ice Age.

Climate does not change rapidly, in a year or two, although it does change far more frequently than some people seem to realise. It is impossible to state a precise time for the beginning and end of the four century long Little Ice Age which gripped Europe from the fourteenth to the eighteenth centuries. For convenience, these dates are often referred to as 1350 – 1750 A.D.,

When:

> *In fourteen hundred and ninety-two*
> *Columbus sailed the ocean blue*

the Ice Age had been tightening its grip for more than a century. The more northerly parts of Europe and Asia (the Norwegian Peninsular, Siberia) and of Britain (Scotland) were in real strife. Islands, such as the Orkneys and the Hebrides, became uninhabitable, as did much of the northern mainland.. Crops failed in Scotland. Farmers struggled to keep their lambs alive in the bitter cold of Spring. Many people moved south, across the border to England or across the sea to Ireland. The Lairds, of course, were stuck. Columbus started a movement which became known, in the 1500-1600s, as The Age of Exploration. They did not simply build better boats and then wonder what to do with them. "Oh, I know. I'll go for a sail around the world." No! They went in search of land where they could grow food to send back home. Having discovered America, the Spanish headed south-west and were rewarded with the warmth (and riches) of South America. The British played it straight and claimed the northern half of America. The French awoke from their siesta a bit late and tried to muscle in on what is today Canada, which the Brits had populated but sparcely. The Brits won – sort of – although parts of Canada are still French speaking and the Trudeau family seems to have a good grip on government. Thousands of people, not only from Britain but also from Europe, made the journey across the Atlantic to take up new lives in America. The settlement of Australia had not yet begun when New Lanark was established, nor had the sponsored migration to Canada.

Against this background of destitution, imagine the joy which must have filled the hearts of the people of New Lanark when Dale and Arkwright decided to build their new mill by the banks of the River Clyde. Work! Work in the warm and dry, not outside in the frozen fields. What was more, it was found that the spinning of the finest yard was best obtained at a temperature of around 80°F. It took decades for the ill-effects of a warm, stuffy, enclosed environment to become apparent. Do not judge the people of yesterday by the standard of knowledge which we have today. I hope I have helped you to understand just how delighted the people of new Lanark must have been to have a house (provided), food, clothes and work in a warm environment.

The first improvement made by Owen was to repair and, if necessary, replace the machinery. This won the approval of both his partners and his workers. He insisted on the factory being kept immaculately clean, himself bending down to pick up any stray piece of cotton he spotted on the floor, handing it to one of the children to place in the bin provided. He then set about improving the accommodation, which was more controversial. More workers necessitated the building of more workers' cottages – no dispute about that – but Owen wanted his workers to have far better cottages than were usually provided. His partners may have been somewhat uneasy in regard to the increased expense coming out of their profit, but the amount was not much and the profits were good so Owen was allowed his way. No. The opposition came from his tenants! They did not object to the better cottages, of course not. They objected to Owen wanting the cottages to be kept as clean as the factory! To this end, he instituted weekly inspections!

Apparently, the men were O.K. with this. Their wives were not!

Gradually, the concept of the landlord providing better accommodation and the tenant taking better care of it became accepted. (I am sure that many of the housewives were already very house proud.) Alcohol was still available – at the other end of the complex – which discouraged the men from carrying too much home. Sobriety improved. Violence decreased – and so did theft. Stealing from the factory had been rife when Owen took over – I presume food, since meals were provided. Owen charged not one person. He simply improved security. People were paid to keep the place clean and tidy, with every item correctly stored on its proper shelf. Those in charge of the shelves made sure no items went missing.

The minimum age at which Owen allowed children to be employed in the mill was ten. Before that it was school time! When Owen took over New Lanark, there were two large stone buildings. When he left there were four. The extra buildings were not for work, they were for community administration and activity, including schooling. Infants were accepted into the school as soon as they could walk, about one year of age, which meant that by the time they started work, they had received nine years schooling. For Owen, education was not about learning facts by rote; it was about expanding the mind. Of course, some things, such as the alphabet and the basics of mathematics, needed to be learned. Apart from that, the classroom was the world outside. Weather permitting (and the Scots were very hardy!) the children were taken outside for walks and their questions provided the topic for the day. A question about a flower might lead to a closer study of that particular flower, to a comparison between that flower and others, to a study of the butterfly or bee that fed upon it – or? If a child asked a question to which its teacher did not know the answer, that was no problem. The class now had a project – seeking the answer. As the schools developed, Owen had large maps of the world placed on the walls to encourage the children to ask questions about other countries. There were also representations of the most remarkable zoological and mineralogical specimens (Silver 1969: 149). The inquisitive mind was the sought-after prize.

There were three levels of education. One assumes the older children gradually spent somewhat more time at their desks, perfecting their skills with the three Rs, but always seeking knowledge was to be a pleasure. No child was ever punished.

It was in 1809 that Owen started implementing his system of education within the community. It was Owen's increasingly obvious interest in education rather than the management of the mill which began to cause problems between Owen and his silent partners, who received annual reports on the state of the business. Profits were still good – increasingly so - but would they not be even better without this unnecessary expense? Owen maintained that the cost of the teaching was born by the local store. When Owen took over, the store had a small selection of items, mostly bought at maximum price due to the small quantity, and sold at an even higher price – for the same reason. Owen took over the purchasing, negotiating far better prices, increasing the range, and adding very little by way of mark-up. The villagers were delighted with the improvement and increased sales ensured increased profit, despite the lower margin. The workers had received increased pay, so there was more money to spend on extras. The profit from the store paid the teacher's salary. Owen argued that the school was not a burden upon the mill but his partners were unconvinced. Adult classes were held three evenings a week; other evenings there were social activities: dancing, singing, whatever brought relaxation and happiness.

In 1806, America placed an embargo on cotton exports which nearly brought trade at the mills to a standstill. Owen persuaded his partners to allow their employees to receive full pay for the duration of the stoppage, which lasted four months (Podmore 1906: 84). It was this act of generosity which finally won the trust and respect of the workers, but it may have contributed to later problems for Owen. I doubt that, when the agreement was first reached, any of the owners had anticipated the embargo lasting quite that long. Be that as it may, Owen's partners started to question the advisability of his philanthropy.

A couple of years later, some of the partners paid a visit to New Lanark to ascertain for themselves exactly what was going on. A little later, a more formal visit was paid. Realising that his partners were not completely supportive, Owen offered to buy them out. According to Packard (1866: 82) the agreed price was $420,000 – again, the amount given in dollars, not pounds. He found new partners but, again, problems arose. It appears to have been a combination of Owen's increasing interest in spending company money on education, combined with his increasingly anti-Christian views, which were the problem. In 1813, he offered to buy out his new partners for the sum of €84,000, which offer was provisionally accepted by the partners who had come to New Lanark to speak with him. However, other partners rejected the offer and the business was put up for public auction. The other partners did not expect Owen to be able to bid against them. Owen, however, travelled down to London, where there were plenty of wealthy people interested in investing in a thriving business. Owen claimed that his former partners tried to keep the bids down by spreading false rumours about the property. If that was so, the plan backfired. The auction took place on 31st December, 1813. Not much interest seems to have been evinced by other potential buyers; the bidding war was between the former partners – and Owen won. Although he (and his new partners) had to pay €114,100, New Lanark was his once again.

An account of Owen's return to New Lanark was given in a letter dated 5th January, 1814, published in the *Glasgow Herald* (Podmore 1906: 100):

> There were great rejoicings here yesterday on account of Mr. Owen's return ... The Society of Free Masons at this place, with colours flying and a band of music, accompanied by almost the whole of the inhabitants, met Mr. Owen immediately before his entrance into the burgh of Lanark, and hailed him with the loudest acclamations of joy; his people took his horses from his carriage and, a flag being placed in front, drew him and his friends along, amid the plaudits of the surrounding multitudes ... his Lady and two of her sisters being prevailed upon to enter the carriage ... the people with the most rapturous exultation proceeded to draw them through all the streets of New Lanark, where all were eager to testify their joy at his return ... Mr. Owen is so justly beloved by all the inhabitants employed at New Lanark, and by people of all ranks in the neighbourhood, that a general happiness has been felt since the news arrived of his continuing as proprietor of the mills. The

houses were all illuminated at New Lanark on Friday night when the news came and all has been jubilee and animation with them ever since.

How Owen's heart must have sung with joy when he compared the reception he was now receiving in January 1814, with that he had received in January 1800. The first half of Owen's life was nearly spent; he was to have many more successes but he was also to have many more failures and disappointments. His triumphant return to New Lanark was to be, perhaps, his most sweet success, with no downside. How many other employers have been greeted by their employees with such joy, enthusiasm and love? I know of none.

4
A New View of Society

The most famous of Owen's new partners was the philosopher, Jeremy Bentham. Four others were members of the Society of Friends (Quakers) with whom Owen's philosophy of life had much in common. The most prominent of these was William Allen, businessman, Fellow of the Royal Society, lecturer in natural and experimental philosophy at Guy's Hospital, a trustee of the Duke of Kent's estates, who no doubt introduced Owen to many influential people, including members of the Royal family.

Owen travelled to London to arrange for the publication of a series of four papers which he had written. That he did indeed do, but at the same time he took advantage of his London visit to seek out new partners, men more sympathetic with his ideas.

By now it was 1813. The four papers which Owen had written were published (quarterly?) during that year and may now be read in *A New View of Society*, published by Prism Press (2013). The precise details of their original publication are not given but each was preceded by a 'Dedication'. The first two *Dedications* are quite short, about a page, but the third and fourth are considerably longer. The name of the person to whom the first *Essay* was dedicated is missing, the first words are '*My Dear Sir*', but Owen refers to the gentleman's position as a senator in the legislator, indicating that he was American.

Twenty years later, Owen was to visit America and endeavour to establish a community there, but this early association with an American was something of a surprise. The second *Essay* was dedicated to the British Public, the third to the superintendents of manufactories and the fourth to His Royal Highness the Prince Regent of the British Empire. In subsequent editions, this became the main dedication.

Essay One expounded Owen's belief that "Any general character may be given to any community by the application of proper means". He claimed that the working class of Great Britain exceeded fifteen million persons, about three-quarters of the population. These people, raised in poverty, were 'taught' (encouraged) by the conditions imposed upon them by society to commit crimes, for which they were punished. The remaining, fortunate, one quarter of the population did not acknowledge any responsibility for the physical or moral condition of these people. "... children can be trained to acquire any language, sentiments, belief, or any bodily habits and manners not contrary to human nature" (p. 22). Humans could only gain happiness for themselves by engaging in conduct which would produce happiness in others.

Essay Two was a continuation of the principals outlined in *Essay One*. It was irrational to be angry with anyone merely for expressing the character which had been imposed upon them by society, let alone punishing them for that expression. Had any member of the upper classes been born into a working class family, they would have developed differently, possibly committed criminal acts. The reverse was also true. Any child born [or adopted] into an upper class family would develop desirable qualities.

Owen described, at some length, Mr. Dale's business which he "sold to some English merchants ... one of whom ... undertook the management of the concern" (p. 37). Without specifically identifying himself, but leaving the reader in no doubt as to who that manager was, Owen then wrote at some further length about the improvements which had been made.

Essay Three addressed the plans in progress for the further improvement of New Lanark, which included the playground to receive children from their infancy, since character was largely formed before the child was two years of age. This was, indeed, a novel suggestion. Never before had the employer deemed himself responsible for the care and upbringing of the workers' children! He spoke of the Sabbath as having being instituted as a day of rest – and *enjoyment.* He reiterated his claim that human beings were not responsible for the formation of their character. He wrote extensively on the importance of the correct education of the children, which did not merely include the 3Rs, but, in the case of girls, learning domestic duties, such as sewing, cooking and keeping a clean house. While war would no longer exist once an ideal society had become established across the world, until that time, boys were to be taught the skills necessary to fight to defend their home and homeland. Nor were adults to be excluded from the process of education. Evening classes were to be made available, if they wished to take advantage of them. The most important task of all was to learn to distinguish truth from error.

He concluded his *Essay* by asking who would accomplish this task? Not, he said, the merchants who were only interested in profit;. not the mere men of law, who were trained to make wrong appear right; not the mere political leaders, governed by self-interest; not the 'heroes' and 'conquerors' who gain their esteem by inflicting misery on others; not those only interested in fashion, still less religious leaders. Then who? Those whose dispassionate and patient investigation had lead them to perceive the truth.

Essay Four addressed to the Prince Regent, later George IV, was titled: "The end of government is to make the governed and the governors happy". This, too, was a novel idea. In times past, the first duty of the King had been to defend the realm, to keep the peace. The latter duty also involved passing and enforcing such laws as were necessary for citizens to live their lives free from the criminal activity of others. The by-product of a successful rule would no doubt have been happiness among the citizens, but that was not the prime responsibility of the ruler. Now Owen was claiming that the *aim* of government should be to bring the greatest amount of happiness to the greatest number of people – including those who governed. This was the aim of those who led tribes of hunter-gatherers. It had been the aim of the Native American tribes, whom he described as "formerly superior" (p. 90). It should be the aim now.

Owen had previously decried the evils of the gin-shops; he now added gambling (State Lottery) to his list of things to be discouraged. And, of course, religious teachings which could not be accepted by all. Rules added by humans to distinguish one religion, one sect of a religion, from another served no useful purpose. Rather they were divisive. As Head of the Church in England, the King of England (or the Regent, during the King's illness) had a unique opportunity, a unique responsibility to act in this matter.

All revenue (wealth) came from one source, and one source only, the labour of man. All should benefit equally from that (communal) labour. The much vaunted and admired British Poor Laws were not solving the problem, they were extending it.

These lectures formed the basis of all Owen's future teaching and work. After he retired from New Lanark, Owen travelled widely, endeavouring to help others set up communities. During that time, many other 'suggestions' were made for their successful running, but they were 'regulations', not principales.

With four of his new partners being Quakers, Owen held back somewhat on his anti-religious doctrines, urging instead acceptance of others' views, without condemnation. Some later insisted that a religious service should be held Sunday morning, to which demand Owen acquiesced, although, of course, attendance was not compulsory.

Among the improved conditions introduced by Owen was one by which medical attendance was provided for all (Podmore 1906: 169). There was also a Sick Fund. Owen had charged parents threepence a term towards their children's schooling, a fraction of the true cost, because he did not want the parents to feel they were receiving charity. It is possible that the Sick Fund operated in the same way? Each employee made a small contribution as they also did to the Savings Fund, designed to provide them with an income in their retirement. Once again, there were problems. This time, the complaints came from the employees, who felt that Owen was overstepping his authority in requiring these deductions to be made from their wages. Some of them wrote, (November, 1823) to the partners in London to register their objection, although Podmore does not record the outcome, merely commenting that, no matter how noble one's intentions, it is impossible to please everyone!

Owen's family grew. Eventually it included four sons, Robert Dale, William Dale, David Dale and Richard, as well as three daughters, Anne Caroline, Jane Dale and Mary. (Their first born son had died in infancy.) They seem to have divided their time between New Lanark and London, Podmore mentioning that the boys received at least some of their education in London, although no details are given. I noticed that the youngest boy did not have 'Dale' as a middle name and wondered if Mr. Dale had died by the time he was born? One of the girls also received 'Dale' as a middle name. It was customary for at least one daughter to receive the mother's maiden name as a middle name.

By mid 1815, the Napoleonic Wars were over. If you thought that with peace came prosperity, think again! Things may have improved on the Continent, but in Britain, trade went into decline. No doubt the King, his Regent, and his Prime Minister, among others, had deplored the cost to the Treasury, but all those boats needed to make sure Britain continued to rule the waves, all those guns, all that ammunition, all those military uniforms, all that food, had to be purchased from somewhere – and that 'somewhere' was British Traders. Suddenly, all that ceased. Furthermore, men employed in the Armed Forces returned home, unemployed. Increased availability of labour led to a decrease in wages. To make matters worse, the summer of

1816 was exceptionally wet and many crops failed. There were demonstrations, even riots. A Select Committee was set up by both Houses of Parliament, before which Owen presented a paper, urging the establishment of self-supporting communities, which Owen had printed in the *Times* and *Morning Press.*

This was not the first time Owen had published information about New Lanark. The four *Essays*, published in 1813, had been penned 1812, during the time of his dispute with his second group of partners. They were probably a putting down on paper of all the thoughts and arguments which were buzzing around in his head at that time. Indeed, the first, addressed to the unknown Senator, may well have been the re-working of an actual letter sent. Now, with his new partners firmly behind him, and a second public exposition of his ideas having been made, 1816 launched another phase of his career, as a public speaker and writer.

On 1st January, 1816, Owen gave an address to the people of New Lanark on the occasion of the opening of the Institute established for the 'Formation of Character'. This was the launch of a project which had long been dear to his heart. The address was later published in a reprint of his *A New View of Society: Essays on the Formation of the Human Character* which he had originally published in 1813. This new version had been considerably expanded. The book ended with some Observations on the Effect of the Manufacturing System. My copy is a 3rd edition published in 1817. I believe the 2nd edition (the first reworked edition) was published towards the end of 1816.

With his new partners' approval, Owen had started to welcome visitors to New Lanark, proud to show them its achievements. Once the stream had started, it never stopped. Up to thirty people a day come, not just from other parts of Britain, but from the Continent, too. In 1816, the Russian Grand Duke Nicholas paid a visit. Other visitors included the Princes John and Maximillian of Austria, Foreign Ambassadors, Bishops and

Clergy, nobility and professional men of every description. In all, the Visitors Book was signed by over 20,000 people.

Owen was asked to make representations before a number of Parliamentary committees as the need for reform within the growing industrial sector became increasingly recognised. Podmore (1906: 209) described Owen as "the pioneer of factory legislation in this country". One group of visitors returned a second time, intent on starting an Infant School in London on the principles recommended by Owen. They asked that James Buchanan, the easy-going schoolmaster of the New Lanark Infant School be allowed to relocate to London, to which request Owen readily agreed. Unfortunately, once in London, Buchanan came under the influence of his wife, not Owen, which meant that the birch was re-introduced! Notwithstanding this set-back, Podmiore (1906: 150) reported that "the Westminster school grew and flourished, and was the parent of many more". I was particularly gratified to read this because one of the partners, Mr. John Smith, banker, was my mother's great uncle.

Much of the summer of 1818 was spent on the Continent, where he met with many eminent people, including Pictet and Cuvier. The year 1821 saw the publication of *The Economist,* a periodical designed to promote Owen's views. The 1820s saw the beginning of the Co-operatives, about which Owen was passionate. These trading stores were intended to make the maximum number of necessary items easily available to the largest number of people. There would be only one brand of each item – the best, if 'best' there could be. It was Owen's opinion that the various brands of goods were pretty much the same, merely dressed up to appear different for the purpose of marketing. With no competition, sales were assured; prices could be kept low. Owen's idea of a perfect shopping trip was 'enter, collect goods, pay, leave' and many men agreed with him. The women did not. They *enjoyed* the challenge of making a choice. Despite these objections, the concept of the Co-operative took hold and there were still some 'Co-operatives' – or "Co-Ops" as they were called - when I was growing up in

England during the 1940-1950s.

Like priests of all religions, Owen's preachings henceforth were extrapolations of the basic tenets of his creed. For example, in *The Book of the New Moral World*, published in 1840, Owen first stated 'five fundamental facts' (principals), followed by twenty 'Laws of Human Nature'. Chapter 7, the longest chapter of the book, addressed each of the twenty 'Laws' with lengthy discussions and conclusions. In *Lectures on the Rational System of Society*, which he published in 1841 expressly to counter the accusations then being made that his teachings were 'socialist' – the term 'socialism' having made an appearance a couple of years before, it is thought for the first time in France. In the first paragraph of that book, he claimed that his 'Rational' system covered all sciences, all ideas, thoughts, feelings, and conduct, of every human being who had ever lived, or would exist in the future. This was some claim, but Owen was the bearer of 'Truth' which was to bring enlightenment to humans who had, until this time, been trapped in 'falsehood'.

I had been puzzled by Owen's reference to 'the millennium', which occurred more and more frequently. I remembered the millennium, standing among the crowd waiting for the rocket to explode in the night sky above to tell us all that 31st December, 1999, had become 1st January, 2000. Why on earth should Owen have been interested in that event more than a century-and-a-half before it happened? He wasn't, of course. The millennium to which Owen was referring was the 'Second Coming'. It had taken early Christians a few decades to realise that Jesus would not be returning in the flesh to bring God's Kingdom on Earth, when sin would be no more. Perhaps they had been mistaken? Perhaps God's Kingdom would come *after* they had repented and reformed? Nearly two thousand years of effort had yet to bring this longed-for event but Owen assured them it was close, very close. Once the rule of Reason had been established, there would be no war, no crime, no dissension. All would be peace, goodwill and harmony. Owen had clearly recognised that his anti-religious views were being counter-productive. He, himself, firmly believed in a Divine, Creative force. He was not being completely deceitful when he endeavoured to engage Christian opinion by offering a similar path towards the Divine.

As his ideas spread, communities were formed and looked to him for guidance. The physical structure of New Lanark had been very simple – three or four rows of houses and four large buildings, very different from the traditional village, with its winding lanes. More importantly, it differed from the alleyways and backstreets of towns and cities, such as Glasgow and London, which Owen came to associate with 'undesirable activity'. All new communities were to be built using a rectangular design: dwellings on the outer rim, with gardens forming the perimeter, one end of the rectangle to house the factory, or other administrative buildings, while the other end was to house the community buildings, designed for education and recreation, especially dancing and music. Owen divided the human life span into four stages, work being allocated according to age, or 'Class'.

First Class was from birth to the fifth year when the child received its first education/training. Children were to be encouraged to express their thoughts and feelings, never to receive any punishment, be fed wholesome food, dressed in light, loose clothing, encouraged to play outside in the fresh air and taught to regard the feelings of others as much as their own. They were to feel no fear but have implicit trust and confidence in those around them.

Second Class was from five to ten years of age. Education continued, as little as possible from books and as much as possible from experience. They would start to help with the domestic arrangements and to work in the gardens and pleasure grounds.

Third Class was from ten to fifteen years of age. As well as assisting with the training of the younger children, these children would increasingly be trained in appropriate handicrafts. They would learn the use of the mechanical devices which were constantly being invented and generally finish their preparation for life as an adult member of the community.

Fourth Class included those from fifteen to twenty years of age, when the children "will become men and women of a new race" (Podmore 1906: 485). They, too, would help in the instruction of the younger classes but this would be the time when they would form a relationship with someone of the opposite sex. There were to be no arranged marriages; each would be free to choose their partner, thus providing the best opportunity for a long, happy marriage.

Fifth Class, those aged between twenty and twenty-five would oversee and manage production of all the community's needs. The younger children had been learning to produce food in the community's gardens for years, as well as learning domestic chores, sewing, repairs, etc.

Sixth Class, twenty-five to thirty years of age, would not be required to engage in production. Rather, their responsibility was distribution. It was thought that this work would require about two hours a day, the remainder of the time being spent in study and social intercourse.

Seventh Class, from thirty to forty, would govern the internal affairs of the community, would settle any disputes which might arise and administer justice – although, I presume, these latter duties would be light.

Eighth Class, forty to sixty years, would be the Foreign Department, charged with keeping abreast of the activities of other communities around the world, learning about new products and organising the sale of their own surplus. They would look after public roads and travel. They would naturally spend much of their time travelling, both for business and pleasure.

As they progressed through life, each person (male and female) would have an equal responsibility and opportunity to fill each role – or class of roles. All could look forward to travel in their (semi) retirement.

On 1st January of each year, every community would hold a meeting, commencing at 10 a.m. At this meeting, every *Class* would submit a report on its year's activities, its successes and its failures. Discussion would be held in relation to the coming year. These reports were to be compiled and made available to every other community in the country so that each might learn from the other. As communities grew abroad, these were reports were also to be available, on request, to any interested overseas community.

Thus every human being, wherever on the Earth they may have been born and raised, would have security of home, food, clothing, work. Their would be no envy of any other community, no jealousy, no greed, no crime, no war. The Millennium would have arrived.

5
New Harmony

How could something which seemed so right go so terribly wrong? Was it indeed the case that if something seemed to good to be true, it probably was?

In 1821, Owen reached the ripe old age of fifty! True to his own 'life diary', Owen turned his attention to promoting his ideas 'overseas', not just Ireland, or Europe, but America. Although Owen's concept of complete equality between all human beings, not just spiritually but materially, was unique to him, along with his antipathy towards religion, people had been living in communities for centuries. These communities – monasteries and convents – had a religious purpose. While the communities held all things in common, they were hierarchical. Indeed. 'obedience' was avowed. They were also solemn. The only singing was that of hymns; there was no dancing; there was little social interaction. 'Communion' was to be with God, not humans. Some monasteries even imposed a vow of silence. Happiness was to be hoped for in a future life, not experienced here on Earth.

That was not Owen's idea of an ideal community! A common purpose – yes, but that purpose was happiness here on this Earth, on this wonderful Earth which the unknown and unknowable Creator had given to us to be enjoyed. Also to be enjoyed was the company of our fellow human beings. Let there be laughter! Let there be joy! Let there be singing, dancing!

There were other groups, other communities, which also had their own ideas. As the Reformation took hold across Europe, various spiritual leaders, such as Calvin, came to the fore. New sects were born, new communities were formed. One such was the Rappites, founded by George Rapp, born in Würtenberg in 1757. To escape persecution, Rapp and his followers fled to America. They purchased five thousand acres of land near Pittsburg, establishing a community which they named Harmony. In a few years these sober, industrious and pious German peasants (Podmore 1906: 285) possessed mills, workshops, a tannery, vineyard, distillery and were self-sufficient in food and clothing.

In 1814, they moved to Indiana, where they had purchased thirty thousand acres, their numbers being now between eight and nine hundred. In addition to dwelling houses, there were four large buildings which would serve as community houses. They grew mulberry trees. The humans ate the berries; silkworms consumed the leaves! This community produced its own silk for weaving.

Now it was time for them to move once again. They needed a buyer – and who better than Robert Owen? In December, 1824, Owen went to America, taking with him his second son, William, his eldest son, Robert Dale, being left in charge of New Lanark. In April, 1825, Owen (with the help of another major investor, William Maclure) purchased all the buildings and twenty thousand acres of land for €30,000. In 1822, a 'Society for promoting Communities' had been established in New York. The concept of communities did not belong to Owen alone. His book, *New View of Society*, was well known. On 25th February and 7th March, 1825, Owen delivered two discourses in the Hall of Representatives in Washington, attended by distinguished persons, including the President. Owen had no difficulty arousing interest in his new project.

Having completed the purchase, Owen returned to England, leaving New Harmony in June and arriving back in England early August. William was left in charge. Owen made several trips between England and America during this time. Should I have said 'Scotland'? I am not sure, because there is no further mention of New Lanark, from which Owen seems to have severed his ties. He had done all he could there; now it was time to expand his vision.

By October of that year, some nine hundred persons were resident at New Harmony. Owen never had an opportunity to choose his early community members. Had he done, he would have selected persons, not only dedicated to his ideas, but ones with the practical skills needed for making the necessary changes. The first, and most obvious problem, was that the community had not been built in the required rectangular formation. Presumably, had Owen had the opportunity, he would have dismantled the existing dwellings, using such material as was suitable to construct new dwellings in the required format and to the required standard. The other major problem was that the former community had multi-tasked. Owen's communities were to be centred around one occupation, be that manufacturing or farming. However, Owen had always proclaimed that *all* were to be welcome. How could he turn anybody away? William had done his best to persuade some of the 'no-hopers' that this particular community would not really suit them, but there were plenty of others, unemployed, often with few, or no, skills, who were desperate to take up the opportunity to start a new life, and how could they be refused?

There were, of course, some people who were just what was needed, but they were insufficient in number.

Inequality in skills was not the only inequality among the new residents. There were money differences as well. Although Owen and Maclure had provided the purchase money, they had little left for changes and improvements. The long-term plan was for the community gradually to buy them out, as it became self-supporting. That would take time – and never happened. The immediate problem was financing. Some of the new members contributed by way of investment. In exchange, they were excused from labour. Others, who had no money, worked. They were credited with the value of their labour. When that reached the investment amount, they would become investors. Eventually, all would become equal; all would share the community work. The community did not last that long.

Certain parts of the community did well: the saw-mill served, not just the community, but the surrounding country as well. Manufactured items included hats, boots, soap, candles, glue. The dye and pottery works were idle for want of capable workers; the cotton and wool mills turned out but little. William wrote to his father on 16th December, 1825 (Podmore 1906: 195-196):

> My Dearest Father,
>
> We were astonished to hear that you had advertised for so many hands, whom you wished to engage as members or hired workmen, for it will be impossible to give them houses, or even rooms here, until we shall have built more houses for their accommodation. Of many of those for whom you advertised we have already sufficient members and excellent workmen.

William went on to explain that they needed (among others) masons, bricklayers, wheelwrights, carpenters, machine makers, potters, cooks, washerwomen and laundresses. William needed them but *"we have no room form them"*. Building houses was, for the time being, out of the question They had no rocks (ready blasted), no bricks, no timber, no boards, no shingles, nothing requisite for building, and as for getting them from others, *they are not to be had in the whole country.* The massive continent of America was far from the same as the little island of Britain! Early settlement had been on the East Coast. Some fine cities were being built there, Boston and Washington, for example. All supplies were flowing *from* the country *to* the cities/towns, not *from* the cities *to* the country.

They needed workmen – not the workmen for which Owen had advertised, but others. They could not employ them because they could not accommodate them. They could not divert labour from other parts of the community because they needed the parts which were operating successfully to keep operating.

What a conundrum!

It is difficult to reconcile the mature, middle-aged man, who clearly had very little understanding of the situation, with the thoughtful youth, who had watched and waited before acting.

There were some aspects of community life which were progressing well. The military was very well organized: Artillery, Infantry, Riflemen, Fusiliers, even a company of Veterans! About 130 children were being educated, the costs off-set by accepting children not residents of the community for a small fee. A Ball was held every week, as well as two concerts. Unfortunately, these activities brought no wealth to the community.

Owen paid a short visit to New Harmony in November, 1825, bringing his son, Robert, with him. After a quick return to England, he was back at New Harmony January, 1826, at which time a general meeting approved a constitution and the organization of the project. There were to be six departments: Agriculture; Manufacture; Literature, Science and Education; Domestic Economy; General Economy; Commerce.

So far, so good.

The traditional religious communities had been held together by their common belief. New Lanark had been held together by the workers' common aim: production. New Harmony was too diverse. The only common bond was the belief that every person had the right to be happy. People made friends with those of similar upbringing, similar beliefs, similar interest, similar skills etc., Soon two separate Societies were formed, each with more than 1000 acres at their disposal, which they asked to purchase. This they were allowed to do. Far from being disturbed by this, Owen was delighted. He planned lots of smaller communities. This was but the start – and it was. Others broke away. The Education Society purchased 900 acres and set up, not only a school, but areas where the boys could learn farming skills, stables, workshops, and, of course, kitchens where the girls could learn domestic skills. The aim was not so much to teach them the 3Rs, or even to incite their curiosity about the world, but to prepare them to be useful members of the community. Today, we would refer to it as a Technical College, or some such. Children were admitted "from birth", not at one year old as previously. They boarded and rarely saw their parents. One such child in later life recalled seeing her parents "twice in two years". (Podmore 1906: 316). Was this what the Divine Creator had planned for humans?

The New Millennium may not have commenced but Owen had announced the start of a New Era. On 4th July, 1826, (American Independence Day), in an address delivered at New Harmony, Owen declared the inauguration of the Era of Mental Independence. Thereafter, the Society's *Gazette* was dated "First/Second (etc.) year of Mental Independence".

Owen does not appear to have viewed the establishment of these sub-communities unfavourably. It had been part of his plan, albeit happening more quickly than he had envisaged. On 6th May, 1827, Owen warned members that any who did not affiliate themselves with one of these new communities would have to support themselves. This resulted in many leaving. In a validictory address given on 27th May, 1827, Owen referred to ten individual communities at New Harmony: Social Colonies of Equality and Common Property. Podmore (1906: 320) spoke of New Harmony 'dissolving' as more daughter communities became established, something which Owen was not yet ready to admit. However, after a further visit to England, in July of 1827, Owen returned to New Harmony in April, 1828 and in address on 13th of that month, admitted that his attempt to establish a community of equality had been premature. Leases he had granted to the smaller communities had been used for personal gain and must therefore be resumed. Those who wished to stay as 'social families' could do so, purchasing their land from him. The last of the land he owned he made over to his sons, all of whom remained in America. In all, the experiment had cost Owen about €40,000.

On Sunday, 12th June, 1828, Robert Owen left New Harmony for the last time.

Owen may have been 'broke' but he certainly was not broken. Right up until his death in November, 1858, he continued to write, lecture, campaign. He travelled widely and met many eminent people. In 1837, while on the Continent, he met with King Ludwig 1 in Munich and Prince Metternich of Austria while in Vienna. On 26th June, 1839, Owen was presented to Queen Victoria, not an unalloyed success since the Queen criticized his opposition to religion and marriage. Owen held that humans were not responsible for their emotions, which came to them unbidden. How could anyone make any commitment with regard to future emotions?

There is no hint anywhere in the literature I read of Owen ever forming a relationship with any female other than his wife, but he did abandon her. After his return from New Harmony, he lived in London, not in his own home, because he could no longer afford to own one. He moved from place to place, according to the kindness of his supporters. There is no record of him having returned to his wife. At that time, she and their three daughters were living in Braxfield, moving to Hamilton, She was struggling to find a place they could afford, having dismissed two servants, intending to keep only two. Of course, Owen had nothing to give her. His sons sent him €300 a month, which they allowed him to think was a dividend from New Harmony, All four of his sons became successful and productive American citizens. His daughters were less fortunate. Podmore (1906: 393) prints part of a desperate letter written by his wife saying how much she desired his advice at a time of great anxiety. His eldest daughter was ill (possibly with tuberculosis?). She died the next month. His wife died the following Spring and Mary, his youngest daughter in the Spring of 1832. The surviving daughter, Jane, went to New Harmony to live with her brothers, marrying one of their close friends and associates, Mr. Flaunteroy. Despite Owen's much vaunted teaching about the equality of the sexes, requiring women to take equal responsibility in the running of the communities, he clearly favoured his sons over the female members of his family.

Those living in communities were becoming known as 'communists'. Robert Owen was undoubtedly a communist, long before Karl Marx, who re-iterated, rather than invented, the doctrine of "From each according to his ability; to each according to his needs". Was Owen a socialist? Yes, said his fellow reformers. No, said Owen.

According to Podmore (1906: 401), the term 'socialist' first appeared in Co-operative literature around 1833, having been used in France the previous year. This is somewhat at variance with the statement made by Podmore (p. 505) that an "Act passed under George III in (1817) Statute 57, had made Socialism, which proposed the overthrow and change of the laws and institutions of the Country, and taught that humans were not responsible for their actions, illegal".

The memory of the execution of Charles I and the 'reign' of the Lord Protector, Oliver Cromwell, was still vivid in the minds of the English and the bloody revolution which had taken place in France at the end of the eighteenth century had shaken them to the core. It is clear from the Statute quoted by Podmore that the term 'socialism' was already being applied to social reform long before it appeared in literature associated with Owen's ideas. It helps to explain why Owen so vehemently denied being a socialist.

Henry VIII may have been overturning a religious authority, the Pope, the Catholic Church, but this was achieved by violence and destruction. The monasteries may have been paid for by the Church, but the beautiful works of art they contained, the statues made of gold, or embellished with it, they had been *made* by people. The melted down gold went into the King's coffers. Of what benefit was that to the common man? Cromwell may have been overturning a temporal authority, but the process was the same – death and destruction. As for the French Revolution – it didn't bear thinking about.

Owen did not want to destroy *anything*. He wanted to build society *up*. He did not want to destroy the beautiful homes of the aristocrats. He wanted everybody else to be able to enjoy beautiful homes as well. He did not believe that the rich were truly happy with their idle lives. He believed that they would find a productive life far more rewarding. He wanted *everybody* to benefit. That was not socialism! "From 1840 onward, Holy War was waged with increasing vigour against the Socialists. At some events, violence broke out – most scuffles, no serious injuries, although some property damage" (Podmore 1906: 518). This was not sanctioned by Owen.

None of the communities Owen had sponsored were successful. The labour exchanges and co-operative stores he founded were. Despite this partial failure, during the last couple of decades of his life, Owen became increasingly 'Messiahanic'. His teachings were the 'Religion of the Millennium' and those teachings were that Man's only duty was to be happy in the world he had been given to inhabit.

In the 1840s, the phenomenon of 'Spiritualism' swept across America and Europe. This involved various means of making contact with (or, rather, being contacted by) departed people. Owen became a spiritualist, receiving messages from those who had gone before (including Benjamin Franklin) assuring him of the worth of his work. Owen, having long abandoned Christianity, had no problem accepting the reality of a far more extended period of creation and with that acceptance came an understanding that he had been misguided in his expectation that the New Millennia could, or would, be established within a decade or so. He realised his work would have to be ongoing after his death.

His health failed him. He suffered from a neurological problem. He became unable to walk, needed to be carried in a chair, and also had difficulty talking. However, his mental faculties appear to have remained sound, as he still attended meetings when he could, although at the last one, he was only able to read the first sentence of his speech, which was completed for him by someone else. Podmore reproduced (pp. 617/623) some of his final letters, the last dated 8th October, 1858, six weeks before he died. The writing is large and shaky but the content was completely lucid.

He returned home – to Newtown. The house in which he had been born was occupied but he was able to rent a room in the adjacent building. He passed on in the early hours of 17th November, 1858. His son, Robert Dale, was with him and recorded that his father knew that he was dying, asking several times what was the time? His last words, uttered quite clearly about twenty minutes before he died were: "Relief has come". He was buried in the local Churchyard, next to his parents.

Podmore (1906: 654) claimed "A place will be found for Owen amongst those whose dreams have helped reshape the world" and I am sure no one will disagree. Podmore wrote more than a century ago. Little did he realise what was to come – and is still coming.

No future reformer had a vision *excactly* the same as that of Owen, but many had ideas, if not visions. What were they? Were they any more successful than Owen in promoting them. Its time to try to find out.

Bibliography

Owen, R. (1813/2013) *A New View of Society*. New York: Prism Key Press

Owen, R. (1817) *Essays on the Formatin of Human Character*. Palala Press.

Owen, R. (1840) *The Book of the New Moral World*. Andesite Press

Owen R. (1841) *Lectures on the Rational System of Society*. Sagwan Press

Owen, R. (1849) *The Revolution in the Mind and Practice of the Human Race*. Franklin Classics.

Owen, R. (1855) *The New Existence of Man Upon the Earth*. Franklin Classics

Owen R., Bellamy, E. and Fourier, C. (2012) *Writings of the Utopian Socialists*. St. Petersburg, Fl. Red and Black Publishers

Packard, F. A. (1866) *Life of Robert Owen*. Carlisle (Mass.): Applewood Books

Podmore, F. (1906) *Robert Owen: A Biograpahy* (2 vols.). London: Hutchinson & Co.

Russell, B. (1975) *Autobiography*. London. George Allen & Unwin

Silver, H. (1969/2009) *Robert Owen on Education*. Cambridge: Cambridge University Press.

6
Far and Wide

In 1905, at the age of 82, Alfred Russel Wallace published his autobiography: *My Life – A Record of Events and Opinions*. It was published in two volumes. Volume I covered the first half of Wallace's life, which had been devoted to exploring. Initially, the exploring was carried out on British soil, collecting and studying plants and small animals, comparing them, trying to establish relationships and differences, a task which turned out to be more complicated than the young lad had anticipated. Wallace was twenty-five when he and a friend, William Bates, set out for South America, where he spent four years in the Amazon. After returning home for two years, in 1854 he set out again, this time spending eight years in the Malay Archipelago, returning early 1862. There were plenty of events to be remembered from those times, including being shipwrecked and drifting at sea in a life boat for ten days!

The second half of Wallace's life, covered in Volume II, was spent at home, in England, with his wife and family. His interest in living things had extended to humans, especially the ways in which they were superior to animals – and the ways in which they were not! He wrote many papers and books and expressed many opinions. Wallace developed a wide range of interests. He wrote on subjects as diverse as the planet, Mars, and the importance (on Earth) of dust! But here it is his interest in social issues which is of importance. He was an avowed socialist and determined to bring about reforms, not only in regard to the ownership or renting of land and houses but also the representation of the people in Parliament. He did not campaign for the abolition of the monarchy or the complete downfall of the aristocratic classes. He was anxious that disruption to society should be kept to a minimum; changes were to be implemented gradually, over a period of up to a hundred years – or more.

Wallace, like Darwin, was interested in theories of evolution. Darwin commenced researching his theory of gradual change by natural means (not Divine intervention) many years before Wallace took up the same idea but Wallace worked more quickly. This eventually resulted in a joint presentation of papers on 1st July, 1858, before members of the Linnean Society, Wallace and Darwin being acknowledged as co-discoverers of the theory of evolution by Natural Selection. (They had exchanged correspondence on this subject.) It seems likely that Wallace's understanding of the slow pace of change in Nature contributed to the patience with which he addressed the problems of social change – social evolution. All other reformers wanted change as quickly as possible. Not Wallace.

Before studying the work, it is needful to study the man.

Wallace was born on 8th January, 1823, in Monmouthshire on the Welsh border. His father appears to have been an only child, his mother having one sister, who had eight or nine children, all but two of whom emigrated to Australia. He never met the two who remained behind. His mother gave birth to nine children, three of his five sisters had died before he was born, aged five months, eight years and six years. A fourth sister died of tuberculosis aged twenty-two. All three brothers, William, John and Herbert (known as Edward), grew to adulthood. The boys were educated at the local Grammar School. The Wallace family came from Hanworth, Middlesex. Of interest to Wallace was the tomb of Admiral Sir James Wallace, although he does not state the exact relationship. Since Hanworth was but a village with a population in 1840 of only 750 persons, all the Wallaces resident in Hanworth could be presumed to be related. His father's name was Thomas Vere Wallace, 'Vere' being the family name of the Dukes of St. Albans, making it more than likely that his family bore some relationship to the aristocracy of St. Albans.. His mother came from the Greenell family, originally from France as refugees, having escaped the massacre of St. Bartholomew in 1572. The Greenell family were financially 'comfortable', his mother's grandfather having been an alderman for a number of years and twice Mayor of Hertford.

The Wallace family may not have been wealthy in the same way that was the Darwin family – Charles Darwin never needed to undertake one day's paid work in his life - but they were not peasants, living hand to mouth. His father qualified as a layer, although he did not need to enter practice, being financially independent at that stage of his life. The suggestions Wallace made with regard to the redistribution of wealth were not the result of childhood poverty, although family finances became straightened following embezzlement of his father's money by a colleague. After this, Wallace's father, and his older sister, Fanny, became teachers. Initially, students were taught at the Wallace home; later the sister opened a small school. His father died at some point, which seems to have been at a time when the oldest offspring were becoming financially independent and were able to support their mother, although his eldest brother died in his early thirties of respiratory complications after catching a severe winter chill. Mrs. Wallace's grieving did not end there. Her youngest son, Herbert, joined Wallace in the Amazon but did not enjoy the wandering life. At port, before boarding a ship home, he contracted yellow fever, and died.

On leaving school, Wallace worked first as a builder, later as a surveyor. This was the only time in his life in which Wallace was in regular employment.

During his time in the Amazon, Wallace had regular contact with several different groups of people – descendants of the original inhabitants, those of Spanish descent, negros (mostly escaped slaves), other Americans and, of course, some British. All were now living similar life-styles in the inhabited areas. Wallace made two expeditions up the Rio Negro and one along a tributary of the Orinoko River, as well as the Uaupés River, where he met a few 'uncivilized' humans. In his autobiography (vol.1: p.288), Wallace claimed that this was his first meeting with "absolute uncontaminated savages". Living their traditional lives as they were, these people were aware of the white man, whom they completely ignored, meaning that Wallace had no opportunity of getting to know them. Things would be different in the Archipelago.

Having 'lost' another son, this time through emigration to the United States, it is hard to imagine the relief and joy Mrs. Wallace must have experienced when the small boat which had rescued Wallace and his ship-wrecked companions finally limped into port, after having been 'missing' for six weeks, or the dismay which she must have felt when Wallace, very quickly, determined to set forth once again, this time to the opposite side of the world. Wallace seems to have inherited his mother's resilience. I am not simply referring to Wallace's determination to set sail once more for distant waters so soon after his unfortunate *physical* experience; Wallace suffered severe *emotional* trauma as well. He had lost everything he had worked for! Wallace had had with him on the ship home thousands of samples of species of butterflies, beetles, and other insects, possibly the skins of small animals and certainly skins and feathers of many birds, as well as some livestock – numerous parrots and parakeets, several uncommon monkeys, a forest wild dog and other creatures. Abandoning ship, Wallace was able to retrieve a small tin box into which he put a few shirts and some drawings, his watch and a few sovereigns. The rest, including, sadly, the livestock, along with three years' journals, had to be abandoned. Wallace claimed £200 from insurance, received €150, and set about rebuilding his life. He gave numerous talks, wrote articles and published small books, which were very well received. Fortunately, he was able to access many of the lengthy letters and journal-style accounts which he had written home – not many relatives, but plenty of friends!

By the time Wallace was ready to depart once more, he was sufficiently well-known and respected as a naturalist to be given free first class passage to the Archipelago. Wallace left England February, 1854. The ship docked at many ports, giving him an opportunity to visit Gibraltar, Malta and Alexandria, before disembarking at Cairo,. The Canal not yet having been built, he made his way across land to Suez (seeing the pyramids on his way), before boarding a boat bound for Singapore where he renewed his acquaintance with Sir James Brooke, the Raj of Borneo. From there Wallace went to Sarawak, arriving November, 1854. Wallace's second adventure had finally begun.

Armed with a letter of introduction from the Raj, Wallace was welcomed in the larger townships by the town's Head Man, who gave him an introduction to another, smaller island, with another Head Man, and so on down the scale. On each occasion, Wallace was accompanied by one or two men from the town/village, who, having safely delivered him, then returned home. Wallace spent time at each place, staying in increasingly simpler accommodation, spending the days exploring the surrounding countryside, collecting samples, much to be bemusement of the villagers, who could not understand why he should be interested in anything so mundane. Some of the small islands Wallace visited were uninhabited and Wallace was able to observe nature at its most natural. Others were home to small groups of people who had never before seen a white man. Wallace was interested in them – and they were interested in Wallace! Many islanders were quite small. Wallace was over 6 ft. He must have made quite an impression!

It was at this time Wallace became increasingly interested in humans, how they lived in their natural state, how they interacted with each other. Wallace always tried to fit in with them, to live as they did. He is one of a very few men ever to have had the experience of living in one of the most 'advanced' societies then known, of experiencing living in smaller cities, towns, villages, right down to a handful of people who had had no experience of 'civilisation' at all. These were not 'one-night-stays'. He remained for at least several days, usually weeks, since he needed that amount of time to explore the natural wonders, the unusual, even unique, plants and animal life. He became accepted, lived as one of them.

By the time Wallace returned home in early 1862, Darwin's book and his exposition of the theory of evolution by Natural Selection were well established. Wallace was content to leave evolution in Darwin's capable hands. He never lost his interest in nature, particularly plants, and continued to study, classify and write about these. But Wallace had been, not so much struck, as bowled over, by the 'civilisation' to which he had returned. The great divide between the rich and the poor had grown to unimaginable proportions. It was not that the aristocracy had become richer – many were poorer – but that more people had become rich – the industrialists, the bankers, the business men. There is only so much money to go around in any society. If some have more, then others have less. The wealth of the rich, it seemed to Wallace, was out of proportion, to the contribution they were making to society. On the other side, poverty had reached a level never before known throughout history. In the past, each community had taken care of their own – helping those in need. Now something new had made its appearance. It was called a 'slum'. People had, indeed, 'slumped'. Hundreds, thousands, of people were living in crowded hovels, some even sleeping on the street. Was this the life Europeans were trying to bring to the 'primitive' peoples of the world. Should not, rather, the Europeans be learning from them?

After his return to England in April, 1862, Wallace became a very busy man. He had brought home with him *thousands* of samples of insects, birds and small animals, all of which needed to be dealt with, one way or another. The work was too much for one person's life time; He enlisted the help of others. He was invited to give talks and met many interesting people. He formed an unlikely friendship with Darwin, but his closest friendship was with Thomas Huxley, who lived nearby in London, where Wallace was living with his sister, Fanny, her husband and his mother. He called on Herbert Spencer, but was disappointed that Spencer had nothing further to offer by way of suggestion as to how life on Earth had begun. He became friends with Sir Richard Owen (Robert Owen's son). Perhaps most importantly, he, along with Huxley, were leading instigators behind the publication of the magazine, *Nature*, which is still held in high regard today. He was a regular contributor.

In 1866, at the age of 43, he married the daughter of one of his friends, Annie Mitten, she being 18 years old. It was a successful marriage. (The age difference was one year *less* than that between my parents, so I know how loving and caring such a union can be.) They had a son, William, and a daughter, Violet.

After John Stuart Mill read one of Wallace's books about the Malay Archipelago, in which Wallace had compared European private ownership of land unfavourably with Malay open ownership, he invited Wallace to become a member of his proposed *Land Tenure Reform Association*, which Wallace did. Mill died in 1871, and the Association died with him, but not Wallace's interest in land reform. In 1880, Wallace, with a group of supporters, formed the *Land Nationalisation Society*, of which he was elected President.

Mill and Spencer had both made one point to Wallace which caused him to stop and think about the possible effects of land reform. If 'The State' owned the land on behalf of the people, who would care for it? The present large land owners expended a great deal of time, effort and money on the upkeep of their properties. Would Civil Servants, with no personal interest in the land, be as concerned for its welfare?

But for the shipwreck, Wallace would have returned to England that first time as a comparatively wealthy man. His thousands of samples would have sold for a handsome sum. Second time lucky. All his goods made it safely to shore. His faithful agent helped him sell many and invested the proceeds for him, such that Wallace received €300 *per annum* in interest, enough to live quite comfortably. Was it because he was kind-hearted or because he wanted money for nothing that Wallace lent more than one friend money to start a business, all of which failed? Wallace tried buying and selling on the stock market. That failed, too. Wallace tried to find employment, but his age, coupled with his lack of business experience, resulted in one unsuccessful application after another.

In 1890, Wallace declared himself a socialist. I am sure this was not something done without much thought. He had personally experienced living as part of a community whose members had virtually no material possessions yet who led a contented life. He had seen how increased material wealth was conducive to greed and jealousy, which resulted in crime and poverty. He was not naïve enough to believe that if everybody had nothing, all would work for the benefit of their neighbour! He recognised that a sense of achievement was an essential ingredient of human happiness, as was the need to feel that one was leaving the world a better place when one died – that one was handing down *something* to one's offspring, even it it was not material wealth.

Clearly, in his middle age he had had no objections to the concept of living on interest received from one's investments. He recognised the need for investment. The days of the village blacksmith or baker were gone. There was nothing in Wallace's book, *This Wonderful Century*, to indicate that Wallace had anything but praise for that century's discoveries and innovations: type-writers, telegraph, photography, etc. Money had been needed, and would continue to be needed, to fund such projects. Wallace strove to be fair and reasonable in all his suggestions.

Wallace had benefited from good investment; he had suffered from bad. He had been wrongfully sued, won a case which had dragged on for years, had been awarded costs, which his opponent failed to pay.. Wallace paid the legal costs himself. Another time, Wallace found that the builder building his house had not paid the workers for two weeks, despite having required payment in advance. Wallace paid the workers himself and the suppliers, sacking the builder and taking over the project himself. Years later, the recalcitrant builder sued him for breach of contract! Again Wallace won; again he was awarded costs; again his opponent failed to pay; again, Wallace paid the costs himself. There was another case where Wallace won a wager (€500). His opponent refused to concede. It all went to Court. Again Wallace won, but his opponent preferred to go to jail rather than pay. Again Wallace paid the legal fees himself.

Wallace wanted society to change. He had plenty of suggestions, not all of which were directly related to socialism. For example, Sunday should be a day of rest for everyone – including staff – even if it meant that householders would need to make their own beds and cook their own meals. 'Rest' meant 'rest from one's usual occupation', not sitting in a chair all day reading a book! Rest was meant to be enjoyable, relaxing, recuperative. For his gardener, gardening was work. For him, it was relaxation. In his *Autobiography*, Wallace said that his greatest pleasure in life was working in his garden. Abandoning orthodox religion, Wallace felt closer to God in a garden than anywhere else on Earth – a feeling shared by Ernst Haekel, whose thoughts we will shortly be sharing.

7
Land Reform

For Wallace, the Government of a country had two functions, and two functions only: the protection of its people from external enemies and the protection of its people from each other. Wallace pointed out that far more people died each year at the hands of their fellow citizens than died as the result of the action of any external enemy. Nor, of course, was death the only injury inflicted by one citizen upon another. Robbery was becoming an increasing problem, especially in the cities. Prosecution was paid for by the public purse; fines went back to the same place. The victim received nothing. Victim compensation is receiving more attention today, but we are still expected to insure ourselves against theft. If a person is uninsured, that is their fault. In the final analysis, does it really make in any difference whether we pay premiums to a company or taxes to the State? The money comes out of our pocket, one way or another.

It was Civil justice which troubled Wallace the most. These cases were mostly about money, a situation with which Wallace was very well acquainted! These cases were 'self-funded', requiring money, of which the aggrieved party may have very little. Only the wealthy could afford to take a case to Court. Legal redress should be made affordable for all. This is a problem which some effort has been made to address through Legal Aid, but it is by no means solved.

Another issue, one to which most of us can still relate, is that of fixed fines. Why should the beggar and the millionaire both be fined the same amount, a possible week's housekeeping for the one, pocket change for the other? I presume that, in times gone by, the maxim: 'The punishment should fit the crime' overruled all other considerations and in the case of crimes involving a prison sentence, may still be the appropriate measure today. However, I agree with Wallace that there are other 'crimes', such as speeding, for which a more appropriate measure would be a percentage of weekly income – the punishment fitting the criminal as much as the crime.

Wallace objected to Trusts which allowed a person to control their money for decades, even centuries, after their death. He allowed that people should be permitted to leave *something* to their descendants, but large amounts of money, in trust, which might attract some form of tax leniency, encouraged the building up of large fortunes within a family and to this extent Trusts may be considered to fall within the scope of socialism, at least as Wallace understood it.

There was one reform which both Owen and Wallace had been equally keen to see brought about. Both agreed that numerous manufacturers producing competing products was wasteful. Money was wasted on advertsing and promotion. One store in each area selling the one product which had been shown to be the most convenient, at the most affordable price, was all that was needed. A period of time should be allowed for products to compete. The most successful one should be adopted. In the same way that great care was taken in sporting events to ensure that conditions of competition were the same for all, so should the same care be taken in business to ensure equality of opportunity. Wallace first used this phrase in an address to the Land Nationalisation Society in 1892. It has since been adopted by many others. All unnecessary and useless occupations should be abolished, which included nine-tenths of all lawyers and all financiers and stock-gamblers. When the remaining labour needs were shared among the population, each person should not need to work more than three or four hours per day.

The rest of the time could, and should, be spent in rest and recreation. Life was meant to be enjoyed. (Hunter-gatherer tribes spend about three-to-four hours a day hunting and gathering. Did Wallace have this in mind?)

The State needed to fund education and training for those unable to pay for their own – to a standard equal to that privately available. In return, the State was entitled to a financial return from those who had thus benefited. Initially, this would still favour the wealthy but Wallace was completely opposed to the inheritance of stocks and shares, which were created as the result of a *private, individual* business decision by one person to lend (invest) money for the commencement or maintenance of some business. If the money lent (invested) had not been repaid at the time of death, it should be treated as any other debt and settled during probate. With 'next generations' not receiving unearned income, to the receipt of which they had contributed *nothing*, the imbalance between the wealthy and the poorer portions of society would become less; state funding for education and training would become more equal and so would any subsequent taxation.

More and more land-owners were turning to sheep farming. Sheep basically took care of themselves, except at lambing time, unlike cows which needed milking twice a day. Wool was in great demand, making two days per year the amount of time each sheep needed individual attention. Unwanted farm labourers were increasingly making their way to the towns and cities where they had heard that factory owners were needing more hands. With more people in need of work than positions available, factory owners were offering very low pay, which was gratefully accepted by those who would otherwise have starved. Wallace supported the socialist call for a minimum wage and also for reforms which we would today call 'Work place health and safety'. Wallace went further. He felt it necessary to fix a maximum income – something I have long felt necessary. Unfortunately, this reform has still not come to pass. On the contrary, the salaries and bonuses paid to CEOs and other top management have reached obscene levels. Sports and entertainment stars are not far behind – if at all. Surely something will be done?

The political reform Wallace advocated referred only to the British system of government, which consisted of two 'Houses'. The Upper House, the House of Lords, had originated from the old King's Counsel. The Lower House, the House of Commons, came into being after the Restoration of Charles ll to the throne and consisted of representatives of 'the people', elected by 'the people' of designated areas, 'electorates'. Unfortunately, 'the people' allowed to vote were very few, originally major land owners. Qualification had been eased a little, but Wallace wanted 'universal suffrage' – at least for men; he made no mention of women, despite having advocated strongly for their equal education.

It was to the House of Lords which Wallace gave his most attention. Some of its members owed their positions simply to inheritance. This had certain advantages. Not needing to be concerned about re-election, they could consider the Bills brought before them without fear or favour. They were not members of a political Party. Also, their attendance was a 'duty'; they were not paid. These men were known as the 'Lords Temporal'. Other members owed their membership to positions in society. They were the 'Lords Ecclesiastical': bishops. That senior members of the Church had an automatic right (duty) to become members of Parliament did not sit well with Wallace! They should go – as, of course, should the Lords Temporal – but the institution of an Upper House should stay. By whom was it to be populated?

Wallace proposed a system of life peerages. Members would be drawn from persons who had proven their ability in society in some way, through their profession, be that business or the arts, such as writing or painting. There would be no campaigning. If they were worthy of election, they would be known in their community. They would be chosen by the local town/district/county council. Once elected, they would be Members for life, thus retaining the best of the previous system while eliminating the worst.

Now, at last, we come to the reform closest to Wallace's heart: Land Reform – or, rather, Land Nationalisation. Among tribal or village peoples, every man, woman and child had an equal right to walk every part of that tribe's territory. That had been the case in England, too, until quite recently. After the Norman Conquest, England had been divided into Dukedoms. Duke's sons became Earls, sub-carers of small portions of the original estate, and so on, down the line to Lords of the Manor, but the peasant people, the villagers, still had the right to walk the meadows, hunt in the woods, fish in the streams, and even walk through the grounds of the Manor House to reach a village on the other side. The enclosure of property had come about when sheep and cattle farming took over from crop farming as the primary source of income for the big estates. Originally, the purpose of the fences was to keep the animals in rather than to keep people out, but things changed over time. Dukes had been but care-takers. They could not sell their property. Their families were tied to the land. With industrialisation, the rise of the 'moneyed class' and the increasing financial straightening of the Upper Classes, estates were being broken up, sold off, pieces enclosed for private use. The land now belonged to 'people' – not 'the people'. That was a denial of a basic human right, a 'right' which had been in place since human beings first came into existence. That 'right' must be restored.

In 1881, Wallace joined in the formation of the Land Nationalisation Society. He was also a founder member of the Land Reform Society. Their concern was not with the nationalisation of Church land. Since the time of Henry VIII, when he not only created the Church of England but nominated himself as its Head, Church land had become the property of the State, of the English people, not Rome. (Henry, of course, was also King of Wales and Scotland but I have never read of either of those countries objecting to having been left out. The Scottish people, for instance, preferred to be Presbyterians.)

In times gone by, the local Lord was expected to provide free accommodation for all his workers. Gradually, the Parish became responsible for Poor Relief and this it did by taxing landowners for each dwelling on their land. The more people the landowner employed, the more people for whom he provided free housing, the more he was taxed! More and more landowners wanted to 'employ' sheep, rather than people. However, the people were tied to the land. The owner could not evict them. The owner may have been responsible for the cost of building the cottage, but, by this time, he had become entitled to charge rent. By raising the rent, he could 'encourage' the tenant to leave, to move to the town. Wallace urged the need for an independent body to be responsible for the setting of rents.

In Scotland, landlords used other tactics. Recovering from the Little Ice Age, which had made much of Scotland uninhabitable, its land desolate, farming and land cultivation was returning. Some Scottish Lords, wanting their land for 'tenant' sheep, not humans, offered alternative land, close to the sea, with access to fishing, beaches to scavenge for shell fish and kelp, cliffs from which to collect eggs and, of course, the land itself – which they would own. Sounded idyllic, and it was, in summer! The bitter winter gales overturned boats, men drowned, leaving families destitute. No fish, no eggs, no harvested crops. Many Scots emigrated either to Canada or Australia. Canada was in particular need of people who could acclimatise to its sometimes harsh climate and some of these people received free passage, offered by those anxious to welcome them, but that did not resolve the inherent injustice they had suffered in their homeland.

The situation in England was somewhat different from that in Ireland and Scotland. Land had frequently been farmed by the same family of tenants for generations. The tenant farmer was often well educated and respected. In England, the tenants were not being forced from their land; they were deserting it. The wages being offered by factory owners in the towns sounded too good to be true – which, of course, they were. No surrounding land meant no free vegetables and eggs. Food needed to be purchased. Time off work due to illness was unpaid. On retirement, one was obliged to leave one's free home and purchase (or rent) another. Poverty was rife, yet the people continued to come. The villagers did not read newspapers; the gossip which reached them was more about the success stories than the failures. And so they continued to try their luck.

Although the situation was different, the solution was the same. People would return if they had right of ownership of their property, even if it were but a small house and but an acre or two of land surrounding it. Wallace pointed out that one or two acres of prime land would be as productive as ten acres of woody or cliff top land. Human beings had been created to love the land they owned, however small that piece of land might be. They would care for it and put it to maximum use – which was what the country needed. Win/win!

Land would belong to the State but each (male) citizen had the right, *once* in his life to select a piece of land, not less than one acre, not more than five, which would be his and for which he would not be charged any money. If he subsequently chose to move, the land would revert to the State and he would be required to purchase his next property at market rate. The property would also revert to the State at the time of his death, although a family member would be allowed to apply for ownership.

Where was this land to come from? Some of it would come from the large Estates. Forward thinking Wallace was anxious to avoid dissent by, and the devastation of, certain sections of society, who were no more responsible for their position in life as inheritor of property than were the poor for not having inherited any. On the death of the Lord, a proportion of the land of his Estate (10% ?) should revert to the State. This land should be around the periphery, divided up into lots suitable to maintain a family. This could be two acres, it could be ten, depending upon the fertility of the soil. Wallace hoped that the poor of the towns and cities would return to the country, where they were needed. The land would be cheap, possibly free, as suggested above. Wallace was certain that the new owners would embrace their property with love and enthusiasm, cultivating it, at the rear with fruit and vegetables, chickens, perhaps a sheep or goat, to feed the family and in the front with beautiful flowers. The Estate may well be enhanced, not devalued, by the presence of these new dwellings. In about another twenty-five years, when the next owner died, another 10% would revert to the State. It would take a couple of hundred years for 50% to revert, but the family should not be too devastated because they would have had plenty of time to become accustomed to the idea. Each generation would be but little affected. Wallace recognised the heritage value of some of the beautiful Manor Houses and Castles. He was not wanting to destroy them, but to contain them.

In summary, there can be no doubt that Wallace portrayed the poor as hardworking and honest and the rich as lazy good-for-nothings. Nevertheless, it is clear that he was not proposing the changes that he did with some idea of reeking revenge on the rich, the rulers. Indeed, he felt that they, too, were victims. Being born to wealth deprived a person of the need to achieve. This 'need' was an essential ingredient of our character building and growth. We *need* to feel proud of our achievements, not in a selfish way, but in a comforting way, a way which allows us to sleep peacefully at night, to approach the end of our life with satisfaction. He wanted to lift up the poor, to level the playing field, without impoverishing or unduly distressing those unfortunate enough to have been born rich. No person was responsible for their birth; none should be blamed.

Wallace mentioned Robert Owen a few times in his biography but never in any detail. He seemed to assume that Owen's ideas were sufficiently well-known to his reader not to need any further explanation. It was this which aroused my curiosity and started me upon this journey. Robert Owen had been dead for half a century, his dream of self-sufficient working communities having died with him, but Owen's sons were still respected members of the community.

Like Owen, Wallace had a genuine interest in the well-being of his fellow citizens, especially those not able to speak up for themselves. The manner in which the two men came to their conclusions cannot have been more different. Owen stayed at home, was interested in manufacturing, changing one thing into another by artificial means, as much for the purpose of making money as for producing goods for the benefit of other people – although, of course, the one could not happen without the other. Wallace travelled as far away as he could from 'civilization', lived as closely as he could to Nature as the Creator had made it, had very little interest in money, other than as a means of exchange for the necessities of life – and, may be, one or two items of comfort – but he had no interest in the accumulation of wealth for wealth's sake.

From these two different perspectives, the two men came to some very similar conclusions. Basically, the best society, the most stable society, was the society in which all members were considered to be of equal worth. Some had more 'gifts' and abilities than others. That was an integral part of the wonder of Creation – no two people were ever exactly the same, physically, emotionally, intellectually, but *none* had chosen the circumstance of their birth or their character. They should feel neither pride nor shame. We enjoy each other's company. We are happiest when we are caring and sharing.

Wallace and Owen may have differed in respect to detail, but they were in complete agreement in regard to principle.

8

The Right to Write

Behind every successful man, it is said, there is a woman – or two - or three (dozen) as the case may be! It was certainly true for Herbert Spencer, who gained his reputation as England's greatest philosopher of the Victorian era (and possibly of all time) in part because he never seemed to lift so much as a finger to do anything for himself. Of course, the wealthy employed many servants (and the not-so-wealthy were very glad of the employment) but what made Spencer different from most other men of his time was that he never married. Even with the help of servants, running a household with many children, perhaps a dozen or more, was a very different proposition from living solo, with two or three live-in female staff, whose sole responsibility was to attend to your wishes.

Not that Spencer enjoyed such coddling all his life – far from it! He was born into a pretty 'run-of-the-mill' family. His father was employed as a lace-maker and also tutored a few boys, Herbert helped out at times with this and at one stage his father suggested creating a small 'live-in' boarding type of establishment that they could run together. That did not happen. Herbert had been a free spirit as a youngster, impossible to discipline. Living a disciplined life himself, as an example to the students, had no appeal. He claimed – or blamed – this characteristic as having been handed down in times past by the female side of his family, who were descended from two families who had fled persecution in Europe at the time of the Reformation. They were devoutly Free Church, rejecting authority, be it by Church or State, upholding the right of every individual to think for themselves, to believe and to act according to their own conscience – and choice! Once established in England, the family became loyal followers of John Wesley, whom they had heard preach in Derby, some of the family becoming ministers. Herbert thus had a religious upbringing, if not an orthodox one from the point of view of the Church of England.

The name 'Spencer' was acquired by marriage into an English 'Spencer' family – not *the* Spencer family. As Herbert Spencer's fame grew, some people did think he was related to the Earl of Spencer. Indeed, one overseas correspondent thought he *was* the Earl of Spencer. Not so. His was an honest, hard-working, upright family, like millions of other English families.

Herbert had been born on 27th April, 1820, under the astrological sign of *Aries*, making him the Ram, not the sheep. He followed no one. He was the first, and only surviving, child of his parents. Their next child, a girl, Louisa, lived 2 years 9 months. The other four brothers and three sisters died at, or shortly after, birth.

Spencer was not an easy child to raise. From his own account, he was not deliberately 'naughty', unlike Darwin, who, in his *Autobiography*, records that he enjoyed playing tricks on others and watching their confusion. Confusion was anathema to Spencer – and to his father, too, apparently. He records how his father always tried to ascertain the reason for everything, which helped form a bond of friendship between the two men as Spencer grew into adulthood. They were not merely father and son; they were firm friends.

But that was in the future. Now he was a carefree lad, who simply did what he wanted, when he wanted. His father, having been a bit the same in his youth, was somewhat sympathetic. Young children are notoriously self-centred. The emotional agony which both his parents must have been suffering as he was growing up, during his mother's repeated pregnancies and the death of eight children (especially Louisa), would have worried him but little. In the end, his parents just could cope no more. His father consulted his brother, William, who had one son, Henry. (Another 'only child'. Was there Rhesus negative somewhere in the family?) And so it was arranged. They would swap children! In times gone by, this had been a common practice, but not in nineteenth century England.. Herbert thought he was going to his Uncle's for a visit and was somewhat put out when his father left without him - taking cousin Henry home with him instead. Herbert left Uncle William's, walking home, which took two days, leaving him exhausted, hungry and defiant (Duncan 1908: 12-13). After a week, he agreed to return and from the age of thirteen, until he was eighteen, Herbert was brought up by his uncle. I suspect the change of heart may have occurred because he rather liked his uncle. They formed a strong bond. Uncle William was his pseudo-parent for the rest of his (Uncle William's) life, although Herbert also formed a strong bond with his true father, who was to be a great help and support in the development and expression of his ideas.

Spencer was slow to make friends, but when he did, the friendships tended to last a life time. A young 'know-all' is not easily tolerated by adult society but as Hebert became older, he became part of that 'adult society'; his right to express his individualistic opinions became increasingly tolerated, accepted and, finally, appreciated.

Home schooled by Uncle William (who was also a teacher, specialising in mathematics), University was never considered for Herbert. Attendance was not expected among families from their strata of society. Herbert's first paid employment was as a design engineer, for which task he appeared to have some aptitude, and for which his excellent training in mathematics stood him in good stead. His practical mind was good at solving problems, such as how a bridge, for example, could be built in this or that particular terrain. However, none of the positions he held lasted very long. When he had completed the design which he had been employed to create, his employment ended. Herbert lost interest in architecture. He wanted to be self-employed, to be able to work when *he* wanted, not when someone else dictated..

In between jobs, he lived with (off) his father, although he also took the opportunity to visit relatives, some of whom lived in the countryside, which he loved. Spencer would happily spend an entire day walking, enjoying the fresh air, the sunshine, the opportunity to rest, to sit, leaning against the trunk of a tree, contemplating life, the universe and our place in it.

Because he never married, he never owned a place of his own sufficiently large to 'entertain'. Always the guest, never the host, this single man was welcomed at many a table, if not for his scintillating conversation, then for his contribution to balancing the numbers of male and female guests at the dinner table.

This was a good time to be alive. Over the past few centuries, peoples' horizons had expanded unbelievably, both physically and mentally. As new lands had been discovered, so had new people, new animals, new plants. Even more exciting than the Age of Discovery was the Age of Science which followed. It was not only gravity which had been 'discovered' (understood), but the steam engine, electricity, photography and, most importantly for Spencer, the telescope and the microscope, the former opening up the realm of the Heavens, the latter a world of life hitherto completely unknown, undreamed of. Spencer read Lyell's *Principles of Geology* published in three volumes between 1830 and 1833, one of the few books he read. He did not agree with all of Lyell's ideas (Heaven forbid!) but he did accept that the Earth was far older than the six thousand years postulated in the Old Testament. The Universe was not merely a few thousand years old, but hundreds of millions. Spencer became smitten with the concept of evolution.

Today, I am fairly certain, Spencer would have been diagnosed as a child with 'Attention Deficit Disorder'. He never could settle to one occupation for any length of time, hence his reluctance to read any substantial books, even as an adult. After a (very) short time at his school work, young Herbert was outside (weather permitting) enjoying a walk, which gave constant variety of scenery, which he found so necessary. Much as he enjoyed being out in the open air, he does not appear to have been over-active. On the contrary – he enjoyed sitting down. Again and again, throughout his life, he records plans for outings, holidays, cut short because he ran out of energy. His health became worse and worse, as it did for most of his friends. When one reads of the medications routinely prescribed, one wonders that any of them lived to old age, let alone eighty-three, the age at which Herbert died. The printing press had been invented centuries previously, but it was the improvement in roads and other means of transport, such as the canals and railways, which allowed books and journals to become readily available to people such as Spencer. While still too expensive for the working man, the cost of monthly and quarterly journals was well within the reach of middle and upper class families – and, l am sure, they would have lent copies around. During Spencer's life-time, the Free Lending Library was born, although it took time to become established. There were journals on just about every subject imaginable and plenty on the topic which interested Spencer most – evolution. Where had the Universe come from? How had it formed? What changes had taken place? What changes would take place in the future?

Spencer wrote a few 'letters to the Editor', with limited success. He then tried one or two articles, with no success. Then, finally, a ray of hope! An editor expressed interest in his work, but asked 'Who are you?" 'Why,' thought the still young Spencer, 'Would you need to know that?' Surely, articles were published on the strength of their content, not upon the reputation of the author? So much to learn! And learn, Herbert did. By the time he had reached middle/senior age, editors were glad to publish anything he wrote; his name was enough to ensure publication; Some editors even asked him to write on certain subjects – but he never did. Spencer wrote what *he* wanted, when *he* wanted. He never wrote at anyone's behest.

As can be seen from the pencil/pen-and-ink portraits drawn by

Spencer of his friends, and reproduced in Duncan's biography, Spencer was quite a skilled artist, as so many Victorians were. It is not surprising, then, that his first paid occupation was as a designer/architect. He received several commissions, each for just the one project, each lasting a few weeks, say three months. Spencer had missed the surge of building which took place during the development of the canals and the railways. Some work was still being done, but many projects which had been completed were not turning out to be as profitable as had been anticipated. Things were in declines, although the pay, according to Duncan (pp.50-51) was quite good. By the time he was twenty-three, Spencer had had enough of (intermitently) working for other people. In 1843, Spencer made a life-changing decision. He would become self-employed. He would become a journalist, join 'the press-gang', as he put it.

One of Spencer's first topics was a 'reply', which Spencer penned in response to an article by Hume promoting the concept of it being the responsibility of the State to educate children. Spencer vehemently disagreed. It was the responsibility of parents to educate their children, an education which would, of necessity, include, not merely the 'Three R's' but also ethics and a philosophy of life. Here one can immediately see the difference between Spencer's view of Socialism and that of many other people. Spencer supported the rejection of the authority of Church and State, in the person of the Sovereign/Monarch. He did not support the replacement of these two sources of authority by a third – a government, albeit composed of representatives of the people, chosen by the people, but whose dictates would be as authoritarian as those of the sovereign had once been. Socialists, such as his contemporary, Alfred Wallace, believed that persons elected by the people would put the interests of those people before their own, that their only desire would be to serve others. Spencer was not so naïve. Those who sort election would be those who sort power.

In March, 1852, just before he turned thirty-two, courtesy of *The Leader*, Spencer published a paper entitled 'The Development Hypothesis'. This was nearly eight years before

Darwin published *On the Origin of Species*. For more than half a century, the topic of evolution had been hotly debated, in the drawing room as well as in the press. For sheer simplicity of logic, Spencer's must rank among the best. Opponents of evolution, those who upheld the doctrine of Creation as told in *Genesis*, argued that those who favoured gradual evolution could provide no proof of their theory, the transmutation of a species never having been observed. Spencer pointed out that the spontaneous creation of a species had never been observed either! He went further, claiming that nobody actually *believed* in spontaneous creation; they merely *believed* they *believed*. Was a new species thrown down from the sky? Did it struggle up from the ground? Did God create it out of clay? How many species were there on the Earth to-day? No one knew for sure, but it was hundreds of thousands, probably millions. Fossils bore witness to the past existence of unknown numbers more. Had all these been created spontaneously? There was as much obligation upon those who thought "Yes" to explain their position as there was upon those who supported evolution.

When did a seed become a plant? At what instant? Was not the transformation gradual? It took nine months for the seed of the ovum to evolve into a human infant; twenty years for it to develop into a man. If development from a single cell into a complex being can take place within a couple of decades, what evolutionary development could not take place over millions of years – little by little? Breeders of both plants and animals knew that the quickest way to foster change was to keep/grow the entity under slightly different conditions – not so different that the entity died but sufficiently different for it to adapt. After several generations of breeding under the changed conditions, the change became permanent. This was known. If such adaptation could take place under domestication, why should it not take place naturally? Lyell's three volume work had convinced many people of the Victorian era that the world of the present was not geologically the same as that of the past. As the environment changed, so, too, did the living forms, both plant and animal – or so Spencer claimed. In later years, Spencer was known for being verbose. Not this time! Darwin took four hundred pages to repeat what Spencer had expressed in four!

Most people were particularly interested in one form of evolution. It may be that of the Universe, the sun(s) and the stars, as people were beginning to postulate multiple galaxies, even multiple universes. Others were interested in the formation of our galaxy, our sun and its planets. Others were interested in the geology of our own Earth, how continents and islands had formed and reformed over time. Others were interested in animals or plants. Some in humans. Some in human societies. Spencer was interested in all, but he gradually became drawn more and more to the study of the evolution of human societies. In other words, he specialised in Sociology. Many people became confused, thinking he specialised in *Socialism*, that new form of politics which was gradually creeping across the western world. Throughout his life, Spencer constantly needed to correct this misapprehension.

Why the mistake? Why the mistake *so consistently*? For the academic, 'sociology' is the study of societies as they exist, noting how they operate, for better, for worse. 'Socialism' is the study of societies, how they operate, for better, for worse – then trying to change the 'worse' to make it 'better'. One is active, the other passive. Spencer was definitely 'passive', except for his writing.

Spencer enjoyed reading journal articles and he enjoyed discussing them with his friends. Initially his 'friends' were his family, especially his father, who had similar interests. Spencer became known for his liking for female company, but his liking was strictly platonic. There is nothing in his biography, anywhere, about any romantic relationship with anybody – of either sex. The biography to which I am referring was written by David Duncan, his secretary. When he turned sixty, Spencer wrote his *Autobiography*, a weighty volume. While he did not expect to live another twenty years, he did expect to live another five, and commissioned his secretary to make notes such that a further single volume could be added after his death to complete his life story. Happily, Duncan, while abiding by

Spencer's instruction not to repeat that which had already been recorded in the *Autobiography*, did summarise Spencer's first sixty years, making copious reference to the *Autobiography*, approximately two-thirds of this single volume being thus taken up. The advantage of this summary over Spencer's own account is that it includes many comments and letters by friends and family about Spencer, giving a far broader understanding of the man than would have been obtained by reading, alone, Spencer's own view of himself. At the age of eighty, Spencer wrote two *Appendices*, the first but brief, describing his physical characteristics more fully than he felt anyone else would do, the second longer, describing himself as a person, which was very insightful.

Journal articles were far longer in those days than they are now. Some were published monthly, but others were quarterlies and it was these which tended to print the longer, more substantial papers. It was usual for many of these journals to print 'Annuals' – a compilation of the year's articles, so that several by one (or more) author on the same topic appeared almost in the form of a small book. Spencer quickly started to compile his writings, expanding/correcting them, as he deemed necessary. Spencer was verbose. He deemed it important to explain everything *thoroughly* to ensure that his meaning was completely understood. The effect was the exact opposite. Reading was often an evening occupation; other members of the household may have been present. Unmarried himself, Spencer had the luxury of choosing whether he spent his evenings alone. Not many other people were so fortunate. Reading was also the expected occupation of gentlemen attending their Club – which many did, especially in London, almost on a daily basis. Membership of such Clubs was limited, only a few new members being elected each year. Later, Spencer was elected to the prestigious Atheneum Club. Reading material was essential to avoid the social necessity of making conversation, if solitude was desired.

Considering that Spencer *boasted* that the only books he ever read were light travel books, why did Spencer assume that everyone else would read his – very lengthy – books from cover to cover? But he did, and his letters were full of complaints about misunderstanding of his meaning due to superficial reading! Herbert Spencer may have been smart, but was he wise? No, I don't think he was. He was dumb about even some of the simplest things, such as understanding that other people might sometimes act in the same way that did he! The caricature of the absent-minded professor reminds us that brains and common sense do not always go hand-in-hand! Duncan (p.27) commented that "despite his interest in the psychology of humanity [about which he wrote extensively], he did not self-diagnose a problem, seeming to accept his feelings as 'normal', just part of his nature." There is even a term which might be used to describe this behaviour – narcissistic!

Spencer's father had died in April, 1866, when Herbert was only forty-six years old. Spencer truly missed his father's friendship, help and advice. He tried to fill the gap by using the services of a secretary – the ever-faithful Duncan. Duncan records that his duties were light. Spencer spent the mornings in bed, possibly reading, a little, writing, a lot? Duncan read to Spencer for an hour in the afternoon, after Spencer's post-prandial nap. The books were books on travel. Duncan read them first. Having selected the reading material, he marked in the margin any piece which drew Spencer's interest, which Spencer might wish to incorporate in a future piece of writing. He was Spencer's companion playing 'rackets', billiards, rowing on the Serpentine, walking in Kensington Gardens. Dictation might be given sitting beneath a tree – not a bad job, if you can get it!

So, in what ways was Spencer similar to Owen and in what ways were the two completely different? Both claimed to be independent thinkers. Both had received a standard 'Christian' upbringing, both rejected Christianity, its authority and influence on Society, but both retained a belief in a Supreme Being, beyond human comprehension. Both rejected the rule of a monarch by inheritance, believing in rule by the people, yet both denied they were socialists.

There was one way in which they were completely different. Spencer was an 'evolutionist', Owen was not.

9
Numbers Matter

You will recall that Owen believed he had received some sort of 'revelation' or 'understanding' when he was but a child. That 'understanding' related to the way in which life should be lived, to the way in which Society should be organised, *now and for ever*. Owen's system was forced to accommodate changes necessitated by the industrial revolution – after all, he was an industrialist and he clearly saw the economic benefits on offer, both for him and his workers. In all other respects, Owen tried to retain the *status quo*. He wanted his system to spread across the world and to remain, generation after generation.

Spencer, on the other hand, accepted but some of the ideas to which he had been introduced (mainly) by his father and his uncle. These he further developed for himself. Like Owen, he claimed ownership of these ideas. If it was pointed out to him that other people, such as John Stuart Mill, had expounded similar thoughts, he claimed ignorance. "Really? I had no idea. I have never read any of his books." He then sort for some point of difference (which there always was) to reinforce his claim of originality. The main area of difference between Spencer and Owen was that Spencer believed in change – constant change. Change may be small and gradual, but it was constant, and universal. Societies evolved as well as individuals.

While Spencer wrote on many subjects, here it is only his views on the evolution of society which are under discussion. So, what were they?

Mention has already been made of his interest in travel. It would be some years before he was able to afford to travel himself, and then but briefly to Europe (mostly Switzerland) and America. The travel stories which truly interested him were those of far off lands, the East, Africa, South America, tribal lands. It was by reading about primitive societies in these far off lands, and comparing them with Western societies, that Spencer was able to trace the evolution of people *as groups*. He noted that when a group was very small, scarcely more than a family, the responsibility of leadership tended to fall where it was most easily shouldered. One person may lead when the activity was hunting, another when it was building the camp, another when the problem was sickness. An older person might lead by giving advice, a younger person taking over the leadership when the advice was being put into action. Age, of itself, did not confer authority, neither did inheritance. As groups became bigger, maybe up to twenty people, or so, there started to be some continuity, both by situation and by family, the parent passing on their special skill to their own off-spring more fully than to the offspring of another tribe member. This was done naturally, for convenience rather than for pride.

Gradually, leadership came to be passed from father to son, not necessarily the eldest son. The father often nominated the son who was to follow him. This prevented discord although the decision was not always followed. History abounds with stories of wars between siblings over inheritance. What Spencer noted was that the very concept of war itself was dependent upon the size of population. Small groups had small requirements, were mobile and flexible. If another (small) tribe was foraging the area from which they had intended to supply their needs, they simply moved on another mile or two. It was when the tribes grew bigger that problems began. More people meant more women and infants, which needed to be carried, assisted, and some belongings, too, I remember from my own studies, that tribes rarely, if ever, exceeded fifty in number, After about forty, there was a tendency for the tribe to split. They would almost certainly remain 'friends', meeting every few weeks or months for 'get-togethers'. Sometimes, several groups met once a year for a big jamboree, at which time exchange of persons of marriageable age took place. Spencer did not mention this in the work of his that I read, although I am sure he knew about it and possibly mentioned it elsewhere. Sometimes groups finally drifted apart, at others they quarrelled and a state of enmity developed where there once had been friendship. Alliances were made and broken, but the point which Spencer was making was that war was dependent upon numbers. If numbers were (very) small, there was no conflict. The pattern was consistent throughout history. At the time Spencer was writing, there were extant groups/societies of all the above types. It was not the evolution of the individual, of individuals within a group, of their intelligence, which determined their manner of living – but the size of their group.

But Spencer had noted something else. The population of Europe was growing, nowhere more so than in Great Britain. In times past, many infants had been born, but great numbers had died within the first two years of their life, mostly from infectious diseases, such as diphtheria, cholera and typhoid. During Spencer's lifetime, great strides had been made in the provision to the general population of clean water and the disposal of sewage and other waste products. Europe's population was growing; England's population was growing. How were people (societies) dealing with this changed situation? The reaction in France and England had been totally different. The last decade of the eighteenth century had seen France torn apart by the French Revolution. The common people had rebelled against their hereditary, autocratic rulers. The death toll had been horrendous. And the result? Another monarch! Known by a different title, Emperor rather than King, but the situation was just the same. Or was it? The new ruler (Napoleon) wanted to extend his rule, which he did, as far as Egypt. His attempts to conquer Britain had been unsuccessful, and had brought much misery to his people. Emperor Napoleon I was followed by his son, Napoleon II. Same old, same old! A brief return to the previous monarch, soon replaced by yet another Emperor, Napoleon III, grandson of the first Emperor. Finally, with his demise, France became a true republic but it was too early for Spencer to know whether this would last.

What about England? Here the reverse had happened. Napoleon had tried to conquer England and had failed. It seemed that the British Empire had grown too big to be attacked and defeated. 'Pax Britannica' was the result, not of a small population, but of a large one. For how long could England and her Empire keep growing? The Earth was a finite size. Was it not inevitable that, if England was too powerful to be attacked from without, she would be attacked from within? This had happened in France – and it had happened countless times among tribal societies. Either peacefully, or with dissension, the need to reduce numbers had been recognised. Where there was space, two tribes took the place of one. Where there was not enough space (sufficient fresh water?) one group may decimate, or even exterminate, the other. This was the fate Spencer believed would inevitably befall Britain, as it had France. In times gone by, there had been small waves, rising and falling. Now the ocean of humanity was bigger, the waves would be bigger. Destruction would be greater. Spencer believed England, the world, was on the brink of apocalypse. He expected the great uprising to take place before the turn of the century and was quite surprised when that event passed peacefully. Spencer died in 1903. He was spared the trauma of witnessing the fulfilment of his prophesy – World War I.

Spencer made one point which I felt was extremely important. The accomplishments of a society are as much, or more, a function of the physical size of the group as they are of their mental abilities. Of course, at least one member of the group needs to visualise a project before it can be undertaken, let alone brought to a successful conclusion, be that project the building of a straw hut or of St. Paul's Cathedral. For example (my example, not Spencer's), were twenty Englishmen to be shipwrecked and marooned upon a desert island, on being rescued ten years later, what evidence would they leave behind of how they had spent their time? Of one thing you can be sure: there would be no replica of St. Paul's Cathedral, or Westminster Abbey – unless you count a castle in the sand.

And so it was, argued Spencer, with the tribal communities which were being found for the first time by European explorers. Who knew what visions one of them may have had, of which he he may have told his companions around the evening camp fire, which remained but an image in that one man's mind? The hundreds, the thousands, of workers employed in the construction of the pyramids, Versailles, etc., etc., would, *alone*, have had about the same ability as the individual tribesman, upon whom the European was inclined to look down, to consider his inferior. Once instructed by White man, native people were just as capable (if not more capable) of the physical work necessitated by major construction. All that was needed was the numbers.

The first book published by Spencer was *Social Statics.* In this, the young, enthusiastic, anti-establishment Spencer supported equal rights for women. Over time, he rather back-pedalled on this issue. He still agreed with the proposition *in principal*, some time in the future. Women, he had found, tended to support existing authority, be it Church or State. If they were awarded the vote, they would be inclined to vote to support the *status quo*, which Spencer was trying to overthrow. If they were allowed to vote, they would impede reform (pp. 138-139). In other words, Spencer supported women being allowed to vote provided they voted the way he wanted! This promise of liberating people, allowing them to express their own opinion, to live a free life, is constantly made by reformers and, time and time again, when the reformer has become leader, he becomes a dictator. I do believe that these people start out with the best of intentions. They just do not understand their own inner nature and desires. But then, do any of us?

10
Developmental Hypothesis

In 1852, at the age of thirty-two, Spencer published *The Developmental Hypothesis*. He was but one of many people writing on the subject of evolution, since the Frenchman, Comte Buffon, and the Englishman, Erasmus Darwin, had both, in the latter part of the eighteenth century, put forward the idea that the Earth was very ancient, millions of years old, and that living things had not been created in six days, but had evolved over countless generations. You will recall that Spencer actually claimed (admitted?) he had read Lyell's three volume work on Evolution, published 1830-1833.

In 1893, forty years – and many, *many*, discussions - later, Spencer wrote a paper on 'The Inadequacy of Natural Selection' which was published in the *Contemporary Review*. He surmised that people would think he had turned his back on Darwinism, but they would be wrong. His paper was written in support of Darwin's *true* theory, which was not the theory being put forward in Darwin's name, increasingly the more so since Darwin's death in 1882.

Darwin's theory of evolution wove together two completely different threads – the warp and the weft. The warp comprised those fixed, longitudinal, threads which pre-determined the width of the cloth; the weft was made up of the threads woven up and down between them from the spindle by the weaver. Which of Darwin's two threads was the warp (foundation) and which the weft? The title of Darwin's book had led people to believe that Natural Selection was the warp and, initially, that had been Darwin's original thinking too. He had started working on his theory in the late 1830s, after reading Edward Blyth's papers on 'selection in nature'. Were 'Natural Selection' to be the only, or even the prime, cause of evolution, changes occurring naturally would need to be of a magnitude such that they would confer a life-saving advantage upon the fortunate recipient. All breeders, both of plants and animals, were aware that, while most offspring bore a remarkable similarity to their parents (more so in animals than plants) occasionally 'sports' did occur, a flower, for example, with double the usual number of petals. However, these were very rare and most spontaneous differences were disadvantageous (deformities). They were not replicated. Over thousands of years, natural variation had allowed animals under domestication to become far more varied than animals in the wild, but all breeders knew that to maintain the changes, the plant or animal must be isolated. Mixed breeding resulted in reversion to the original type, which happened in nature.

Lamarck had postulated that evolutionary change took place gradually *in complete populations* in response to changed environmental conditions but his theory had been rejected. Spencer was rejecting Darwin's early thinking, which he claimed Darwin also rejected as his theory evolved. Darwin later held that evolutionary change came about due to the inheritance of *acquired* characteristics – acquired, that is, during the life-time of the individual. The most well-known example put forward was the strong arms of blacksmiths, who acquired their great strength over their life-time. This additional muscular strength was passed on to their male children.

I doubt very much that Spencer ever read *The Origin*, although certain paragraphs may have been read to him. I doubt even more that he ever read *The Variation of Plants and Animals under Domestication*, published by Darwin in 1868. In this work, Darwin wrote extensively on the subject of *pangenesis*.

Body cells replicated – that was universally agreed. Darwin proposed that cells threw off 'gemmules' which circulated throughout the body, eventually combining together to form the reproductive cells. If a body part altered in any way during the life-time of the individual, for whatever reason, that change would be recorded in the gemmules and, therefore, passed on by inheritance to the off-spring. It was easy to disprove Darwin's theory. Twenty-three generations of mice sacrificed their tails, yet still baby mice were born with their full tail in tact. For thousands of years, Jewish males had suffered circumcision, yet each male child still needed the operation. Darwin never answered these criticisms and Spencer seemed unaware of them. By the time Spencer wrote his article (1893) the fact of evolution was almost universally accepted, except for a minority who held to the story of Creation as told in *Genesis*.

A firm believer in evolution, Spencer rejected the Creationist view. What other choices did he have? Spencer was no atheist. He accepted the existence of a Supreme Being, beyond human comprehension who was ultimately responsible for everything. Whatever had happened, had happened with that Being's consent. But what had happened? If spontaneous mutation at the time of birth was insufficient to account for all the beneficial changes which had not only occurred, but which had been sufficient to account for the survival of those individuals over that of their companions, then what other option was available? In Spencer's opinion, only one. Changes occurred during the life-time of the individual and these were inherited by their offspring.

Every individual was capable of sustaining some change in their physical make up over the course of their life-time and many individuals in a community might well undergo a similar change – longer legs, thicker fur, etc., etc. Spencer did not rule out completely the possibility of sudden change due to 'sporting'. He merely stated that this was insufficient to account, not only for all evolutionary change, but even for the majority of it. Any role it played was but subsidiary and this, insisted Spencer, was the conclusion to which Darwin had come. His paper had been written with the intention of supporting Darwin., not condemning him. In response to the article, Huxley wrote that he had no *a priori* objection to the transmission of modifications. Indeed, he would rather like it to be true.

Of what, if any, significance was this for Spencer? Animals (and plants) exercised no control over their own evolution, and neither did humans – or, at least, neither *had* humans, up until now! Things were changing! Now humans had greater understanding, they could influence their own path, physically, mentally and socially. The blacksmith had always known that he could increase his strength by increasing his physical effort. He now knew that his efforts would not only benefit him, but would benefit future generations of his off-spring. In times gone by, the education of women had been deemed unnecessary. Darwin had recommended that women in their prime child-bearing yeas (18-24) should be subjected to intensive education. The stretching of their intellect would result in any children born to them possessing improved intellectual abilities. Indeed, the possibility of improving the intellectual capacity of all citizens was a strong consideration when parliamentarians voted to make education compulsory for all, not only girls as well as boys, but poor as well as rich. Furthermore, the State took on the responsibility of paying for the education of those who could not afford to pay for their own. Darwin's theories were, indeed, changing the world.

While Darwin had primarily been interested in the evolution of the individual, Spencer was interested in the evolution of groups of individuals – of societies. These, too, need no longer wait for natural change to occur. We could study the various stages of development of societies, the positives and negatives of each, make decisions, make changes to harvest the best and discard the unwanted.

It was not only the 'fittest individual(s)' who should, could and would survive. It was the 'fittest' societies. Societies comprised not merely dozens, or hundreds, even thousands of individuals, but *millions*. What greater calling could there be than the improvement of society – the improvement of the life of every single human being.? The joy to be experienced upon witnessing the happiness and welfare of one's fellow human beings would more than compensate for any reduction in personal wealth which might be experienced by the few.

11

Social Socialism

Persons who were avowed socialists were intent upon replacing rule by monarch and aristocracy with rule by the people, or, rather, by representatives of the people whom the people had freely chosen. The concept of a parliament of elected representatives to advise the monarch had been a reality in Britain for eight hundred years but the people eligible to be elected, as well as those eligible to vote, were very restricted. Spencer was unconvinced that those who sought the power to govern by election would necessarily be any more compassionate than those who ruled by inheritance. It was the passing of laws itself which was the problem, not the means by which they were passed. 'Every step away from individualism is a step towards socialism' (p.300). It was for this reason that Spencer so ardently denied that he was promoting socialism. It was the lack of an agreed definition which caused the confusion. The problem was human nature. 'You do not sufficiently bear in mind the *organic* badness of any society organized out of existing human nature ... there is only a certain amount of liberty of which men having a given nature are capable, and if a larger amount of liberty is given to them they will lose it by organizing for themselves some other form of tyranny' (p.301).

Spencer had always demanded for himself the maximum amount of freedom to act as he wished but he recognised that some people's 'wishes' might be detrimental to others. Owen had believed in the innate goodness of humanity. Those fortunate enough to be able to grow up without being corrupted (as would happen in his societies) would remain kind and thoughtful to the end of their days. Spencer sought the minimum amount of control compatible with the maintaining of order and studied other societies in the hope of finding the answer. Smaller societies were definitely more caring towards each other but had limited amounts of capabilities. The very word 'civilised' meant 'town dweller', coming from the Latin '*civic*'. Its extension to mean a large number of people, living under one form of government, was inevitable, since the one cannot be had without the other. Spencer opposed laws to improve ventilation in people's houses because he opposed interference by government in peoples' homes; he opposed measures designed to prevent cruelty to children because they might interfere with the parents' right to discipline their children as they saw fit (p. 303). Had Spencer read more widely, he might have learnt of Buddha's 'Middle Path'!

Alas, by 1892, when Spencer was but in his early sixties, it is clear that all the attention and approbation that he was receiving was beginning to turn his head. Not only did he oppose legislation designed to protect children from cruelty, he also opposed certification of nurses. He considered this proposal to be restrictive, both of the freedom of the individual nurse and of the employer in being able to choose whosoever *they* desired to perform the task of caring. It was 'a restriction upon individual liberty to which I am strongly opposed ... certificating a nurse ... cannot secure sympathy and cannot secure unwearying attention' (p. 315). A certificate cannot make a doctor caring either, but surely he realised the necessity there of training, so why not for a nurse? It could be said that his position was consistent with that which he had held since his childhood – individual freedom. But what did Spencer think of the individual? At that time, Spencer also wrote: '... little or nothing can be done to check the increasing drift towards socialism ... unhappily, the English people, and perhaps more than others the middle classes, are too stupid to generalize ...

The results are too remote and vague for their feeble imaginations.' (p. 314). And further, speaking of Irish Home Rule: 'In my early days I held the unhesitating opinion that self-government was good for all people, but a life passed in acquiring knowledge of societies in all stages has brought a decided change of opinion. The goodness of these or those institutions is purely relative to the natures of the men living under them' (p. 315).

Like Owen before him, and many other political reformers after him, Spencer assumed that people given freedom of thought and action would think and act as did they. As the fiftieth anniversary of Owen's death drew near, a memorial was being organized. Initially, Spencer declined to be involved, but later changed his mind. It was his opinion that '... large though Owen's claims may be in the way of achievement, he lacked a trait which I think essential – he was not sincere. He did not say candidly what he believed, but tried to please both parties. The scientific world and the religious world' (p.325). While it is true that Owen did try to find common ground between Church, State and people, the claim that Owen did not say candidly in what he believed can only have been made by someone who had never read Owen's works!

The best summary of Spencer's thinking was made by himself in a letter to J. A. Skilton, 10th January, 1895 (p. 366):

"If, as it would seem, you think that I have got a scheme for the future of society in my head you are altogether mistaken. Your conception of applied sociology – a bringing to bear of evolutionary principles on social organization with a view to its improvement – is one which I do not entertain ... You have faith in teaching, which I have not – you believe men are going to be changed in their conduct by being shown what line of conduct is rational. I believe no such thing. Men are not rational beings, as commonly supposed. A man is a bundle of instincts, feelings, sentiments, which severally seek their gratification, and those which are in power get hold of the reason and use it to their own ends ... There is no hope for the future save in the slow modification of human nature under social discipline. "

l came to the end of my study of Spencer's work with a sense of sadness. So much potential, but how much of it was fulfilled?

There is no doubt that Spencer was gifted with a great intellect. His family upbringing enabled him to avoid being brain-washed by the accepted doctrine of his time (Adam and Eve and the six days of Creation) despite the family's Weslyan affiliation. Many people were interested in evolution and much was being written, but Spencer's *The Development Hypothesis*, published in 1852, was among the best. Darwin accepted Spencer's term 'Survival of the Fittest' as being more appropriate than 'Natural Selection', which term implied some form of deliberate/ conscious decision by some force or entity. Spencer's assessment of the expression of human character within societies was unique and very insightful. He recognized that (very) small groups were essentially peaceful; somewhat larger groups could be aggressive if they needed to be to protect their land from other, similarly sized, groups. Even larger groups, not feeling threatened, became peaceful again, and so the see-saw continued, throughout history, all over the world. He also recognised that it was only necessary for one or two people in a community to be imaginative for great things to be created – provided there were enough persons in the groups to provide the necessary muscle power. Help was needed, either willingly given, co-oerced or forced, if necessary by capture and enslavement. It was all a numbers game. No group or nation of people was better or worse than any other – simply in a different stage of development, according to their number.

These insights came to Spencer while he was still a young man. Then he applied the brakes on his own mental development. He refused to read other people's work, other than small portions which he had reason to believe might contain some point of interest, against which he could argue. He never wrote anything in support of anybody else. He refused to write any article upon a requested subject. If other people were already thinking about whatever it was, then he was not interested.

Spencer expected other people to read his publications, yet never read theirs. Spencer expected support and acceptance of his opinions yet never supported the opinion of others. Of this he boasted. I have never read of another scholar such as he, and, I have to confess, I hope I never do!

Was Spencer a socialist? That all depends upon the definition applied.

Spencer died in 1903. For practical purposes, we may say he lived and worked during the nineteenth century. During that time there was no political party standing candidates for Parliament, either in Britain or overseas. Each parliamentarian was elected upon his own abilities and appeal. The bloody French Revolution may have deposed France's King, but he had been replaced by an Emperor - and an Empire – one that reached, not merely across Europe to Egypt but into French Indo-China as well. No sign of 'Socialism' as we understand it today. The Americans had replaced their hereditary monarch (George III) with a short-term monarch, one who could 'reign' for a mere eight years, but who, during that time, had far more political power than had any British Monarch since the Restoration in 1660 under Charles II. Not only was their President actively involved in party politics, indeed was elected by one of the two major parties, he could sign 'Executive Orders' which overrode the wishes of either, or both, Houses. This power continues to this day. 'Republican', 'Democrat', yes, but not 'Socialist'.

Britain, too, developed a two-party political system, 'Conservative' and 'Liberal'. 'Liberal' had nothing to do with the freedom of the individual. It promoted the concept of free trade. The Conservatives were happy to allow the import of such items as cotton, provided the import helped British industry – and its exports. Free Traders wanted to be able to import cheap items, particularly from the East, for direct sale in Britain, in competition with home produced items. Neither party had a 'social' agenda as its foundation. 'Socialism' as we understand it today, simply did not exist.

So what was 'socialism'? There was no precise definition but the term was generally applied to those who wanted to change

Britain's social structure in some way. Spencer – as far as I am aware – never wrote a word of criticism about Britain's monarchical system, neither did he criticise the privileged position of the aristocracy. Why would he when he so enjoyed their generous hospitality, his walks on their estates? Not keeping a 'home' of his own of sufficient size to welcome visitors, he, himself, became the eternal visitor, moving from one Estate to another, as a welcomed guest. Single men were needed to even up the numbers around the dinner table! What Spencer objected to was Law, be it Divine Law as promulgated by the Church or Human Law, as dictated by Parliament and Councils, both County and Local (Parish).

I feel the most telling act of Spencer was his refusal to support Government legislation designed to reduce cruelty to children. Why would a person, who so vaunted his love of children, behave in this way? Spencer's own explanation was that such legislation might impede a father's right to discipline his own children. From where had this right come? Spencer may have rejected Christianity but he held a firm belief in the Divine and he clearly believed that Man (or, at least men) had a Divine right to make their own decisions when it came to deciding how they would live. If he had invented a slogan, surely it would have been 'You can't tell me what to do!' Spencer wanted to curtail the power of parliament. Inasmuch as this would involve a radical change in the social structure of society, Spencer was a 'socialist'.

12
The Cream at the Top

In 1971, Daniel Gasman published the first edition of his book, *The Scientific Origins of National Socialism*, the culmination of the research work he had undertaken for the submission of his doctoral thesis. In 2004, a second edition was published (reprinted 2007). This second edition contained a lengthy *Introduction*, which, not so much supplemented, as superseded, the original *Preface*. Unless otherwise stated, all page numbers cited refer to this second edition of his book.

In his *Preface*, Gasman had explained that he did not consider that the *scientific* underpinnings of National Socialism had been sufficiently appreciated, let alone studied. His *Preface* was short. The following paragraph is my understanding of Gasman's understanding of Haeckel's position.

In times gone by, the doctrine of 'Free Will' had implied that people were free to think and act as they chose. During the nineteenth century, the mind, as well as the body, was being studied; Ironically, as it was becoming appreciated that not all animals were 'automatons', behaving instinctively in predetermined ways, but some at least had a measure of reasoning power, it was also becoming appreciated that humans did not possess as much free will as they had always assumed, but often (frequently? usually?) behaved in predictable ways, according to their emotions and the situation in which they found themselves. The study of interactions between the non-material (mind) and the material (body/environment) became known as *psychology*. Psychology was a science; not an exact science as were mathematics or physics, but approaching more the degree of biology. Two people may eat the same meals; one may put on weight, the other may not. Sometimes, physical bodies appeared to behave in a similar manner in similar situations; at other times, they did not. Was not the same true of the mind? There was an underlying similarity between all human beings; there were also innate differences, which ensured that no two people were precisely the same, physically, mentally, emotionally. Theories of evolution were now portraying Man, not as a special creation, made in the image of God, but as an advanced animal, with animal propensities. Few animals lived solitary lives; most lived in packs, herds, flocks, groups organised in some way, in the *same* way, according to their species. Was there not a 'template', a model, after which all human societies should be formed, allowing humans to live in peace and harmony with their fellows, without crime? For millennia, this had been addressed as a philosophical question, subject to debate and discussion. During the nineteenth century, it came to be seen as a scientific question. All life on this Earth, in this Universe, was subject to the Laws of Science, of Nature. There were no exceptions.

We have seen the great importance attached by Herbert Spencer to the structure of societies, which he acknowledged were different at different times, in different places, under different circumstances. In this he differed from Robert Owen, whose approach was 'one size fits all'. Spencer was known as a philosopher; had Owen been asked, I am sure he would have designated his approach 'scientific'. For Haeckel, a 'philosophy' which was not 'scientific' was no philosophy at all.

The young Gasman was a student during the 1960s, a time when the world had recovered sufficiently from the horrors of the Second World War for an attempt to be made to understand its origins. In his original *Preface*, Gasman claimed that the Nazi doctrines had been based on science, at least 'science' as it was understood by them, that science being 'the survival of the fittest' theory of evolution as propounded by Charles Darwin (*On the Origin of Species: 1859*) and as taught by Professor Ernst Haeckel, Germany's most famous biologist. Haeckel was a devout believer in Darwin's theory of evolution by Natural Selection, which clearly taught that those who survived, propagated and flourished, were those who deserved to do so. Clearly, no creature *chose* the body into which it was born. There was a strong element of luck, of favour. Whose 'favour'? There was an increasing movement towards replacing 'God' by 'Nature' or, at least, considering them much the same thing, which seemed to be the position increasingly being taken by Darwin himself, although he tended to vacillate.

Gasman mentioned Charles Darwin and Darwinism without explanation, assuming his readers knew sufficient about the topic to make further extrapolation unnecessary. I feel, however, that to understand Haeckel (and Hitler) it is necessary to acknowledge the statement made by Darwin at the end of Chapter VI of *The Origin*: ' ... let the strongest live and the weakest die'. These few words sum up Darwin's teaching. Nowhere in his book did Darwin refer to the evolution of the human race, but others did. His staunchest supporter, Thomas Huxley, published *Man's Place in Nature* in 1863, a mere four years after the publication of *The Origin*, and that book was devoted to the evolution of humans from apes, from monkeys. Darwin's 'let the weak die' applied as much to humans as it did to any other living entity, plant or animal. Darwin never disputed Huxley's claim of human decent from the ape family, which had previously been made by Lamarck (1809). His own book, *The Descent of Man* (1871), did not address the issue; it simply suggested a fanciful scenario of possible early tribal life *after* humans had become established. It was replete with tales of men killing others perceived as rivals – even their own sons.

White Europeans took it for granted that they were superior to black Africans and Australians, most of whom were still living either nomadic lifestyles or had but simple wooden huts for dwellings. The brown inhabitants of South-East Asia were somewhat more advanced, as were the people of India and the yellow races of China and Japan. These people were educated (or, at least, their upper classes were – and that was all that was educated in European society), but they lacked the technological knowledge of the Europeans, who clearly had better brains. But were all Europeans equal, the same? Clearly not. Haeckel, who was himself fair haired and blue-eyed, considered the tall, Scandinavian people of the north to be far superior to the short dark people of southern Europe, the past histories of Rome and Greece notwithstanding. There were blond, blue-eyed people living in northern Europe, such as the Danes, the Dutch, and people of northern Germany, who might not be quite such fine examples of physical manhood as the Scandinavians, but who surpassed them in technological achievement. These people had reached the pinnacle of human evolution. Haeckel referred to all of these people as 'Nordic'. There was a popular conception of an 'Aryan' race, which may have originated somewhere in the East. No scientific evidence has been found for such a race and this concept has faded away. However, it was frequently referred to in Haeckel's time and the Nordic race was the 'Northern European' branch of these mythical people. The people we refer to today as 'Scandinavians' are the only blond haired, blue-eyed people on the face of the Earth, all others having brown eyes and auburn, brown or black hair. At some time in the past, a genetic mutation clearly did take place. That much must be acknowledged. What must be questioned is how much, if at all, did this mutation make these people different from/superior to, other human beings *in essence*?

Haeckel completely rejected the concept of a personal God, who took an interest in human affairs, at times intervening, but he did accept that there must be some unknown force which had brought the Universe into existence. There were not 'Ten Commandments' – only one and that was the one Darwin had stated so clearly in *The Origins*.

Haeckel was a sincere man, who strove to live his life in accordance with that which he believed to be the purpose of our existence − improvement of the race. Individuals did not have a purpose − only groups. Haeckel's writings were, of course, penned in German. It was to Gasman I turned for an in-depth study of Haeckel's work, his thoughts and how they effected the society in which he lived.

Ernest Haeckel was not merely a biologist. He was a *renowned* biologist. During the first half of the nineteenth century, the Frenchman, George Cuvier, had excelled in his understanding of anatomy − not only human anatomy, but that of animals as well. It was said that his understanding of the inter-relationship of any bone with that of its immediate neighbours was such that he could reconstruct a complete skeleton by studying the remains of a single bone. He studied not only the shape and size of the bone itself, but areas of muscle attachment, from which he deduced size, shape (and purpose) of the muscle which would have been attached, which led him to deduce the size and shape of the next bone − and so on. Now Haeckel was bringing a deeper understanding to physiology, especially the working of the soft tissues. Advancement had been made possible, not only by improved microscopes, but by changes in legislation which allowed bodies to be donated to science for dissection and study, *post mortem*, both in the healthy and diseased condition. Humans suffer far more disease than do animals. The earlier dissecting of animals had greatly increased human knowledge of basic anatomy/physiology, but the understanding of pathology was now possible in a way never before known.

It was Haeckel who coined the phrase 'ontogeny recapitulates phylogeny'. All life started as a single cell. Hours, days, weeks, months later, it had become a multi-cellular being, capable of independent life (although possibly in need of help in the early stages). Study of aborted human foetus had shown that, at some point, the foetus had a small tail. There were also indications that the foetus 'breathed' through gills, as do fish, the lungs being a later development. Attempts to identify specific extinct species as having been distantly ancestral to humans have now been abandoned but it is still accepted that we can deduce something of humanity's path of evolution from these findings, in a general way.

I am sure Haeckel would have been aware of the various theories of evolution which were current in the first half of the nineteenth century, both in Europe and Britain, but it was Darwin's theory of evolution by Natural Selection which gripped his imagination. Born in 1834, Haeckel was but twenty-five years old when *The Origins* was published in 1859. He had completed his medical degree and chosen his path as a student of the new science of biology. The times, they were a-changing. More and more people were questioning the literal truth of the Bible and with that questioning came a loosening of the hold the Church had upon every aspect of human life – and death. Early Christians had not adopted the Egyptian belief in the necessity of preserving the exterior of the body for all time to allow the soul to continue to survive after death, but they had placed great importance upon the need for burial in sacred soil, near a Church. The body was not allowed to be devoured by wild beasts, as were those of other creatures. No! The complete body was carefully wrapped, placed in a box and lowered into the ground. Years later, behold! The flesh had disappeared! If it was no longer in the box, where had it gone? Possibly to heaven, to be re-united with the soul? Did not the Bible state that "in my *flesh* shall I see God"? There was no precise Church teaching upon this point, although the reunion of body and soul was expected 'On the Last Day'. Left behind were the bones, the dead bones, not considered to be 'living', as was the flesh. After two hundred years, these bones could be dug up, disposed of, and the burial plot used again – which is why the same grave yard was able to be used for so many centuries, without ever becoming full.

With the medical; profession now able to study, first hand, the anatomy of the human body, 1858, saw published the first edition of the best-known medical book ever written, *Gray's Anatomy*. What a time for Haeckel to complete his medical studies, to become a qualified practitioner! After a short time in practice, Haeckel took up a teaching position at Jena University, where he remained for the whole of his working life, studying and teaching, becoming a Professor, and gaining the (justified) reputation of being Germany's greatest biologist.

Darwin's book was published in German in 1860 and Haeckel was among the first to read it. The attraction of Darwin's theory was, for him as it was for many other people, that evolution did not rely upon the intervention of a personal God, but upon an eternal, unvarying process, dictated by 'Nature', which had no favourites. This was science!

The Laws of Nature were amoral – not *immoral*, but *amoral*. They were neutral, unchanging. All religions had been created by humans and should be discarded. The word 'religion' comes from the Latin *'relegere'* – to rule. Haeckel clearly saw that promoters of religion were endeavouring to rule people's lives by claiming some form of divine authority, a divine authority which differed from time to time, from place to place, from person to person. Animals recognised no divine authority but lived ethical, amoral lives in accordance with the eternal Laws of Nature. Humans should do the same. No worship was necessary, for there was no one to worship. As Haeckel's doctrine, which he called 'Monism', spread, it came to be considered a religion, and within this context, it was.

In Nature, there were the rulers and the ruled. There was dominance and submission. That was the only way life could continue, both within and between groups. Haeckel was no egalitarian. Equal opportunity – maybe. Equal result – never! Haeckel did not believe in hereditary authority, passed down generation by generation, either by right of 'blood' or position. It was necessary that some people should rise to the top, but that rise should be the result of ability. How right was Darwin! The 'fittest' should survive. As for the rest, Nature would deal with them in due time. Charles Darwin's cousin, Sir Frances Galton, proposed eugenics, which was adopted, but rarely practised, in America and Germany. England flirted with the idea, but eventually rejected it. Haeckel did not actively canvass this thought although some of his followers did.

Like Spencer, Haeckel took note of various human societies. With the easy going societies of warmer climes, where less effort needed to be exerted to obtain the sustenance necessary for survival, there was less labour – and less division of labour. In colder climes, such as northern Europe, not only was more effort needed from each individual, more co-operation was needed. As societies became larger, leaders became more dominant. It is possible that Haeckel was aware of the work of Herbert Spencer, after all, he was an academic, albeit in another discipline. However, he would not have needed any input from Spencer to come to the conclusions he did. Both men accepted Darwin's theory, although, of course, Spencer was older by the time *The Origin* was published. Society was divided as to whether native people should become more like Europeans or Europeans become more like natives. Haeckel tried to bring the two sides together, to combine the best of both worlds to form one perfect one. Hard work, struggle, they were essential for improvement. Leadership by ability, not inheritance, was also essential. The weak, the sick, the poor, would gradually disappear. He did not suggest killing them. That would not be necessary. The State would not waste its resources on those who were of no use.

In his *Preface* to the first edition of *Scientific Origins*, Gasman explained that the aim of his work was to show the scientific underpinnings of the political movement which later became known as National Socialism, in particular the role of biology. Biology unites, not only the two disciplines of anatomy (structure) and physiology (function), but also those of zoology (animals) and botany (plants). It was not normally associated with politics. However, when National Socialism morphed into Nazism, it most certainly did.

Gasman commenced his work by reference to the year 1859, which he referred to as the *annus mirabilis*, not only because, just before its termination, Charles Darwin's book, *On the Origin of Species*, was finally published, but because earlier that year John Stuart Mill had published *On Liberty* and Karl Marx had published *Critique of Political Economy*. I think it is worth while adding that the publication of these three influential and thought-provoking books in this one year, is evidence of the willingness of the people of that time to expand their vision, to consider new ideas, not just scientific (industrial) but philosophical. Before the end of the century, in 1898, Wallace had published *This Wonderful Century,* drawing attention to the extraordinary number of inventions which had occurred during that century: the bicycle, torpedo, sewing machine, type-writer, photography, telegraph, mail service for 'ordinary' people, submarines, x-ray, anaesthetics, electric lighting, the list goes on and on. I feel that to understand Haekel, it is necessary to understand the world in which Haeckel was living. The Age of Exploration had astounded Europeans by its discoveries, new lands, new creatures. Now Europeans were discovering wonders on their doorstep, beneath their microscope, at the end of their telescope. There was a sense of optimism in the air, such as had probably never been experienced before in human history. Owen had felt it, just its beginnings. Spencer had sat back and admired it. Haeckel ran with it.

Haeckel called his philosophy *Monism* in acknowledgement of the one 'substance' from which the Universe had emerged, both matter and energy, body and consciousness. The world appeared to be dualistic: good/evil, positive/negative, hot/cold, up/down, male/female, but this was its outward expression. Its *essence* was but one. Through lectures and articles, Haeckel's philosophy spread across Germany, and into other countries of Europe, especially France and Italy, over the last three decades of the nineteenth century, but it was not until 11th January, 1906, that the Monist League formally came into existence.

The nineteenth century brought great riches but it also brought great poverty – a trend which is continuing to this day, with the rich getting richer and the poor getting poorer. What was the answer? God alone knew! The best Christianity could offer was to cite the words of Jesus: "Woe unto the world because of evil! For it must needs be that evil come; but woe to that man by whom it cometh!" (Matthew 18: 7).

The changes which overtook society during the Industrial Revolution are impossible to enumerate. Much is made of the liberating effect of the railways but there was another liberating change which occurred much closer to home. Clothes became readily available! In past times, clothe was spun at home. Wealthy females acquired a new outfit once a year – remember, it was hand-made and decorated. It was worn for the first time, along with a new hat (the famous 'Easter Bonnet') on Easter Sunday and became the 'Sunday Best' for the following year. Next Easter, it was relegated to 'everyday wear'. A further year later, it became 'work wear', at some point being handed down to staff, who wore it for a few more years, as it gradually made its way down to the peasants in the fields. One outfit a year would not keep the cotton mills turning. For the first time, 'everyday wear' was manufactured and this was soon followed by 'work wear'. Can you imagine the excitement this must have caused among the general population? Factories brought *huge* benefits, especially for the working classes, who no longer needed to rely on cracked and chipped hand-me-down crockery. But these benefits came at great cost – not financial, but social. Before electricity became available, the factories were powered by steam. The furnaces needed to be maintained seven days a week.

In earlier times, *everybody* (including those living in the Manor House) worked extremely hard at certain times of the year – sowing and harvest time – but in between, labour was less. There was plenty of time to celebrate 'high days and holidays', i.e. Saint's Days, as well as Christmas, Easter, Ascension Day, Whit Sunday. There were literally dozens of saints' days, more than a hundred, Catholics celebrating more than Anglicans or Protestants. The term 'Protestant Work Ethic' came into being in acknowledgement of this difference.

While some people in society concentrated only on the benefits brought by industrialisation, others were aware of the associated disadvantages. Many people were aware of both, but felt helpless to change the situation. A few tried to put their thoughts into action, tried to maintain the benefits where they could while seeking to mitigate the associated problems. These were the visionaries of their time and it is Haeckel's vision which I am trying to uncover, to understand.

Haeckel was born 16th February, 1834, in Potsdam, from which town his family relocated to Meresburg, where his father worked as a government lawyer. As a child, he developed a great interest in botany, keeping, not one, but two, herbaria. It should be noted that in the days before radio and television, most children kept small creatures (caterpillars, ladybirds, mice) and/or small plants, which they cultivated and nurtured as their hobby. However, not all children kept two herbaria, one for 'true' species', which could be classified according to text book criteria, and another for those that appeared to vary in some way. Whether or not species were invariable, or whether they were subject to spontaneous variation in nature, free of human interference (domestication), was a matter of serious debate, a debate Darwin attempted to settle when he wrote *On the Origin of Species*. Also hotly debated was whether or not all human beings were of the same species, merely different varieties/races, or whether there was more than one human race: black, white, yellow, brown or even more? It was not until the twentieth century, with the advance of understanding of reproduction and the role of chromosomes, that the simple test of inter-fertility or inter-sterility provided a simple criteria, although even that was not absolute. There are, for example, some pigeons which can interbreed with other varieties, but those varieties cannot interbreed with each other.

Strange as it may now seem, it was not until the Age of Industrialisation that Europeans undertook any serious attempt to change the natural world around them – its plants and animals. Before then, the world was accepted as God's creation, unchangeable in essence. Occasionally a plant or animal was born, or grew up in some way which differed from its fellows – known as a 'sport'. These were usually 'one-offs', a subject of interest while they survived (which, in the case of an animal, might not be for very long). Most such variations, especially in the animal kingdom, appeared to be disadvantageous. Deliberately choosing a deviant, deliberately trying to breed from that deviant by crossing it with a close relative, which sometimes produced another deviant, was a novel activity, which caught the imagination of the wealthy, who had the time and money to expend on such an enterprise. It was into this mental climate that Charles Darwin and Ernst Haeckel were both born and which problem/potential consumed their thinking throughout their entire lives.

13
Monism

The decade from 1856 to 1866 was one of great change for Haeckel. Not only did he graduate from student to teacher, from physician to zoologist, he became a citizen of a new country. The demise of the Napoleonic Empire had left Europe in a fluid state. During the first half of the 1860s, Bismark rose to power, waged war against Austria and succeeded in uniting a number of former Saxon/Teutonic/Germanic states into the new North German Confederation. Not all of the former small states joined the new Confederation, much to Haeckel's regret, but it is interesting to note that those which did join together were the northern states, which would have been home to the greater number of blond blue-eyed citizens. Haerkel embraced the visions of both Darwin and Bismark and it was to the practical uniting of these two philosophies that Haeckel devoted his life.

In 1860, Bismarck launched his life's work – the unification of German States. In 1866, he obtained his objective. Thereafter his time and energy were taken with maintaining and promoting his achievement. The same could be said of the work of Haeckel. It was in 1860 that he first read Darwin's book, *On the Origin of Species*. It was in 1866 that he published his two volume work, *Generelle Morphologie*, which Gasman described as being "his most elaborate theoretical statement" (p. xl). In it Haeckel "attempted to subsume all of science under Darwinian principles and guidelines" (p. xl).

Gasman made the excellent point that, while France and England both had had centuries of history behind them, under the rule of single monarchs, this had not been the case with Germany. The independent states had been bound (loosely) together by the bond of blood – intermarriage between their rulers. Like most families, they squabbled, took sides, changed sides. The coming together of many of these states into the one Confederation was the *commencement* of a truly German history. During the period of establishment, strong leadership by the rulers of the State was needed. This was no longer the case in either France or England. In France, the monarchy had been overthrown, replaced by a 'democratic' Emperor(!), whose dream had been a unified Europe, ruled over by Napoleon and his heirs, a dream Bismark was finally terminating. In England, the monarchy was in the safe hands of Queen Victoria; England's brief flirtation with Republicanism, under Cromwell, had not worked out well. Since that time (1649-1660), England's rising wealthy and well-educated middle class were showing themselves quite capable of managing their own affairs, including those of the Estates which they owned. 'Democratic, socialistic liberalism' meant something completely different in those two countries from the meaning which it held in Germany. The desired end was the same: maximum freedom for the individual commensurate with the strength and welfare of the nation. It was the means by which this end might be achieved which differed.

Haeckel's opposition to Christianity appears to have stemmed from two fronts. Firstly, he was non-religious. Haeckel never denied the existence of some Creative Force but he considered that Force or Energy to be completely beyond human understanding to the extent that it was a waste of time and effort to attempt to grapple with it. Furthermore, this Force, whatever it might be, had no personal attributes, had no personal interest in any human, in humanity or in any living entity. How and why the Universe had been created was not for Man to know. Secondly, there was a constant struggle for power between Church and State. The Pope may no longer rule over the whole of Christendom but where Protestantism had replaced Catholicism, other religious leaders had replaced the Pope, and some were even more authoritarian. Only Man could rule over Man, and that man, or those men, should be chosen by those over whom they ruled and to whom they would be answerable.

There was a problem. Nature was not democratic – or, at least, not for much of the time. A herd of cattle, slowly munching its way across the grassy plain, each caring for its own calf but no other, might be an example of a democratic community, but not the pride of the lion. Nor was there anything 'democratic' about the lioness stealing and killing the deer cub as soon as it had been born or the spider winding its thread around the hapless fly which had been caught in its web. Looking to Nature to learn the rules of the Universe, rather than to a book written by Man, was a commendable concept but it was a concept hard to apply in practice. One thing was clear. Be it a herd of cattle or a pride of lions, each was loyal to its own and had no compunction in regard to fighting, or even killing, a member of an opposing unit.

Gasman (p. xli) identified three streams of thought which combined to provide the material for Haeckel's philosophy: romantic idealism, scientific positivism and materialism, and Darwinism. Fully to appreciate the impact of these ideas, it is necessary to try to understand the thinking of people in preceding centuries. For nearly two million years, our ancestors had lived as any other zoological species. They built a home, found a mate, obtained food and raised offspring. Humans first deviated from the standard pattern when they started to cultivate food in large quantities, a task which they undertook in groups, producing more than was needed for their immediate sustenance. This had two consequences. The first is well acknowledged; they became less mobile, more settled. This settlement had another consequence: it reduced the general knowledge of most individuals.

Hunter-gatherer tribes may travel hundreds of miles over the course of a year, timing the passing through of their territory with the changing seasons as different foods becomes available for consumption. The person farming the one piece of land may never have travelled more than a few miles from their home in the course of a life-time. They may never have seen another species of butterfly, bird or beetle inhabiting an area not so very far away. Of course, there were always travellers, traders, who brought back with them tales of places far away, which might, or might not, have been believed. Those living in mainland Europe would have been less effected than those living on the island of Britain, or those living in the desert areas of the Middle East. It was these narrow bounds which allowed the idea that 'that which is now is that which has always been' to grow and flourish. How the world was then, in their life-time, was how it had been when first created by God.

The Age of Exploration opened many eyes. Some of those 'tall tales' had been true. There were plants and animals – and people – such as they had never imagined. In the eighteenth and nineteenth centuries, the idea of evolution had been put forward by people such as Maupertuis, Count Buffon, Lamarck and Erasmus Darwin, Charles Darwin's grandfather, but these had been rejected by the Church as being contrary to biblical teaching. Nevertheless, the idea of change was becoming established as more and more fossils of no-longer-living species were being uncovered. All exponents of evolution attributed these changes to the Will of God. Charles Darwin's book made scarcely any mention of God, suggesting that change had occurred 'naturally'. At last, those people who had been increasingly chaffing under the yoke of Christianity felt themselves able to speak out against it, with scientific backing. A wind of change swept across, not only Britain, but Europe, where Darwin's book was speedily published, read and accepted.

Despite being 'all-encompassing', Darwin had not taught equality. Rather the reverse. Individuals of a species, be it plant or animal, were not all equal. Some were superior to others and would thrive, while those which were inferior would disappear. This applied as much to the human species as it did to any other. Darwin carefully avoided making reference to people, to suggesting that one race or nation was superior to another, but the inference was clear.

Thus it happened that in the very year that Bismarck commenced his political campaign for the unification of the Germanic States, Haeckel read Darwin's book. This serendipitous co-incidence laid the foundation for the rest of Haeckel's life and work. The inter-relationship between God, the Church, the State and the individual were being questioned in a way they never had been before in the whole of recorded human history.

Gasman (p. xl) made the important point that, while in the longer established kingdoms of France and England, it was *personal* freedom which was increasingly being emphasised, in the newly established kingdom of Germany, it was the freedom of the *State* which was of foremost importance. He felt it significant that the left-wing political Party called themselves 'National Liberals'.

In 1859, Haeckel visited Italy. His tour of this historic country fuelled his love, not of Italy, but of Germany. His letters record how, everywhere he went, viewing the evidence of their past and glorious history, he was consumed by a love and admiration for the modern Germany. In other words, he was homesick! This is not an unusual situation, but in Haeckel, it appears to have been extreme, igniting a 'nationalistic narcissism' which remained with him for the rest of his life. Animals had a social life – so did humans. Animals' social life was organised according to their needs – which were for their safety and well-being. These being adhered to brought harmony within the group, although they might need to unite to fight for their group survival. This was as true for humans as it was for animals.

Haeckel held a life-long belief in spontaneous generation, which may seem strange to the modern reader. This fact is noted by Gasman (p.10) in the paragraph following the one in which he had written of Haeckel's innovative work on one-celled organisms, of which he described one hundred and fifty new species. Half a century earlier, the French scientists, Lamarck, who, in 1809, had published the first full-length exposition of the theory of evolution (three volumes), was the first person to describe single-celled organisms. Lamarck claimed that all life on Earth had evolved from these single-celled organisms. The laws of Nature being unchanging, if life could arise spontaneously in a single cell *once*, then it could do so again – and again. The alternative was to suggest that it had been a 'one off' event, never repeated. Lamarck rejected this concept, but believed that spontaneous generation could, and did, occur in single celled organisms – *only*. He did not believe in the spontaneous generation of birds, mice and maggots and other small creatures, as many people did. In defence of our ancestors, I must point out that to the dweller in the countryside, birds appeared every spring and disappeared every winter. No one knew where they went, or from where they re-appeared. It was not until explorers began exploring Africa that they found those missing birds enjoying the African sunshine while Europeans were shivering through their winter. Problem solved! (Where do flies go in the winter? I don't know. Do you?) Haeckel held the same belief as Lamarck in relation to the spontaneous generation of life in single-celled organisms.

In earlier times, most art had been religious in nature - men and angels, saints and sinners. Haeckel painted pictures of single celled organisms and other 'simple' entities (p.11), seeing painting and poetry as forms of worship, which he encouraged, both bringing the individual creating the picture or the poem closer to the creative power of Nature.

In the same way that Darwin had become one of the most widely read authors in England, Haeckel became one of the most widely read in Germany – and, indeed, Europe. I will cite but one example given by Gasman (p.14). In 1899, Haeckel published *Riddle of the Universe*. During that year, it sold more than a hundred thousand copies, ten editions were produced over the next ten years, and it was translated into about twenty-five languages. Popular acceptance did not necessarily mean scientific acceptance and many criticised/rejected Haeckel's ideas.

Haekel's 'homesickness' during his early visit to Italy did not deter him from further visits to other countries. Now secure within himself, he visited "every corner of Europe, to the tropics, Asia Minor, North Africa, and the Arabian Peninsula" (Gasman, p.19). Like Darwin and Wallace before him, Haeckel was awe-struck by the majesty of the unspoiled tropics, their majesty, their quietness, their stillness, their unending silent life.

In the same way that Darwin had been torn between viewing the Earth as an incredible creation, breathtakingly beautiful, and looking beneath the surface grandeur to observe death and destruction, so, too, was Haeckel torn between amazement at human (especially German) achievement, particularly the technological achievements of the previous hundred years, and the breakdown of moral values, which he perceived happening throughout society. This undermining of core values was leading Germany (and humanity) towards inevitable disaster, social collapse. Monism was not merely the 'icing on the cake'. It was the very 'staff of life' itself. That Monism came to be seen as a religion was not surprising, since Haeckel preached its principles with religious fervour.

In accordance with the Judaic tradition, Christianity taught that Mankind was a special creation. Not so, taught Monism. All living creatures came from the same source. For some, this elevated animals to a status similar to that of humans. The 'animal rights' movement had begun. There was another consequence – not one taught, or apparently sought, by Haeckel. In the eyes of some people, humans were brought down to an animal level, especially in regard to sexual relations. Male animals take sex whenever they can. Why should human males be any different? The fact that many (if not most!) female animals keep mating to a necessary minimum was conveniently 'over-looked' as females were encouraged, too, to become more sexually liberated. As said above, this was not part of the Monist doctrine, but it was a consequence.

The Secular Humanist movement, which was becoming established alongside Socialism, emphasised this position and may have been one of the reasons Haeckel expressed his dislike of 'socialism', although his anti Church, anti Establishment attitude in all other areas could be, and was, associated with a socialistic approach to life. For Haeckel, there was a distinct difference between 'socialism' and 'socialization'. While Humanists inflated the role of the human (albeit in an atheistic universe), the Monists recognised the Earth as but "a tiny grain of protoplasm" (p.33), humans being of no more importance than any other part of Creation. This was in accord with the Gospel teaching that God cared as much for the birds of the air and the flowers of the field as he did for people, which teaching tended to be preached on Sunday but forgotten by Monday.

Human existence might be 'equal' with that of any other living thing, be it plant or animal, but individual humans were not equal, nor were societies or races. Individual inequality was found throughout Nature. Darwin's meticulous work had shown that even birds, which looked identical to the human eye, differed in the length of their beak, of their claws, their feathers, their weight. No two were ever absolutely identical when studied in sufficient detail beneath the microscope. It was upon these differences that evolution by selection relied and those differences were manifest in the mental and emotional areas just as much as they were in the physical. In the same way that the group was more important than the individual in the herd or the flock, so the State was more important than the individual. It was the duty of the individual to support the State, not of the State to support the individual. Dying for one's country was a duty, not an honour. As for the sexes, equality was preached, but it was an equality of worth, of regard, not of role. The two sexes were different, physiologically and emotionally and were to fulfil different roles in society.

In relation to crime and punishment, Haeckel thought more attention needed to be paid to the personality (mental state) of the perpetrator. This should be taken into account, as well as the nature of the crime itself. He recognised that those of low or defective intelligence should not be considered in the same way as those of normal or higher intelligence. He suggested young offenders being trained in a trade. Most of his suggestions are today standard procedure, but he made one suggestion, which has yet to be adopted, one which I have privately considered to be the best solution for many years. In the case of moral offenders, especially those who attacked children (paedophiles), he recommended that they be housed in institutions which would become their permanent home. These places must be provided with farms. workshops, schools and churches. Men and women should be housed separately, to prevent reproduction. Sexual deviants have some form of 'quirk' in their brain. They cannot be cured by medicine or by counselling. A few, with a minor problem, may wish to change their behaviour and seek help. For them counselling may be of assistance. For the rest, it was a waste of time. However, a prison cells was not the place for a person with a mental disorder. 'Secure' villages needed to be built, completely self-sufficient. Let them be 'deviant' with each other, if they so desired. At least they would do no harm to anybody else.

Unlike any other religion then known, Monism rejected the concept of the soul, in humans, in animals, in any form of life. Later, Humanism, which also rejected the concept of a soul, was to become recognised, legally, as a religion, but that was more for the purposes of claiming tax exemption than it was a matter of philosophy. Haeckel's criticism of Christianity traced its descent from its earliest, benign, beginning, sometime after the (supposed) death of the (supposed) person, Jesus, of whom there were no contemporary records, through the rise of the power of the Papacy, the increasing wealth of the Church and the decreasing wealth of the people, who were expected to accept a promise of future happiness in heaven to compensate them for their present earthly sufferings.

Fortunately, Haekel's writings and correspondence were not destroyed, but remained, untouched, in the archives at Jena University, where they were able to be accessed by Gasman after the re-unification of Germany. Gasman wrote another, longer, book, *Haeckel's Monism and the Birth of Fascist Ideology*, which was published in 1998. The first two chapters rounded out Gasman's account of Haeckel's work and ideas. The remaining nine chapters were devoted to the work of Haeckel's supporters, both in Germany and throughout Europe.

In this book, Gasman drew attention to the fact that the main article of Haeckel's faith was not new. On the contrary, it was the oldest philosophy known: there was one universal divine source which had created, and now supported, the entire Cosmos. Energy and matter emanated from the one source; it was their manifestation which differed. All was one – one was all. 'God' was not to be found within the confines of a building, however 'sacred'. 'God' was 'out there' – in the fields and the forest, the sky and the stream. Humans saw the organic and inorganic, the living and the inert, but every atom was alive with God's energy. This calls to mind the statement made by Christ that if the crowd held their peace 'the stones would cry out' (Luke 19: 40).

Haeckel rejected the Christian concept of the individual 'soul'. There was one, universal 'soul', from which all took life and consciousness. At death, that 'energy', that 'soul;', would return to its source. The 'individual' did not survive death; energy did. That was eternal. There was a constant cycle of life and death. Haeckel taught that the 'energy' would live again in another form but he did not teach the reincarnation of the individual.

The purpose of Creation was beyond human understanding but by studying the Laws of Nature – how Nature *worked* – humans could strive to live in accordance with those Laws. No person could do more. No person should do less. This applied as much to groups, societies and nations, as it did to individuals. Alas, one could not look to Nature to ascertain Man's correct social behaviour because the behaviour of social animals differed so greatly. Spencer endeavoured to overcome this obstacle by studying native people still living their traditional lives but even this was fraught with difficulty. They differed, according to the circumstances within which they lived. Haeckel fully realised that the German society of his day could not – should not – try to replicate that of their earliest ancestors, or even that of their more recent, pre-Industrialisation, forebears. Societies, as well as individuals, evolved, adapted as their environment changed.

The individual must be strong, not merely for his own benefit but for the benefit of the group, the society, the nation in which he, and his family, lived. If I had to choose a society, or rather a group of societies, which might have influenced Haeckel's thinking, I would choose that of the ant and the bee – insects whose life-styles Darwin wrote about at some length in *The Origins*. The individual of those societies was of no worth, other than for their contribution to the group. Many did not even reproduce. Haeckel wanted *all* women to reproduce, divorcing and remarrying if their first union was unproductive, but it was not the happiness of the individual with which he was concerned. It was the welfare, the growth, of the State.

Of Haeckel's supporters, the best known today would undoubtedly be Mussolini. If it seems strange that a brown-eyed, dark haired, Italian would embrace Haeckel's Monism, it must be remembered that 'survival of the fittest' was but one factor in the equation. Another factor, a more important factor, was the belief that it was Nature which laid down the rules of Life, not 'God'. Darwin may have vacillated in his beliefs regarding the Creation of the Universe, the involvement, if any, of the (presumed) Creator in our everyday lives, but others of his followers held firmer views. After Darwin's death, the agnostic/atheistic/humanistic interpretation of 'Darwinism' became increasingly prevalent. Nowhere in the world was the influence of the Pope, the hold of Christianity, felt more strongly than in Italy. The (known) world was still ruled by Rome, but through a Pope, not an Emperor, by Christian, not military, 'soldiers'. It was the overthrow of established religion, of Christianity, of the Pope, which was attractive to many of Haeckel's non-Germanic, non-Nordic, supporters.

The after-effects of the fall of the Napoleonic Empire were felt in Italy as they were in Germany. In earlier times, the Italian isthmus had been ruled by a number of noble families, each with their city of governance – Rome, Florence, Naples, Venice, Milan. As a single country, Italy was as new as Germany. What was unusual was that Vatican City remained independent, ruled over not by an earthly prince, whose succession was handed down by inheritance, but by a divinely appointed prince, known as the Pope, who had recently declared himself to be infallible! Being independent, being a Church, this State paid no taxes to the Italian government, although its citizens were free to come and go throughout Italy, using its roads, railways, hospitals, shops, etc. Talk about the best of both worlds! It is not surprising that a movement took hold seeking, not so much freedom *of* religion, as freedom *from* religion – fascism. The National Socialism of Germany and the Fascism of Italy both grew in the soil of Darwinism, but they grew from different seeds. They were political movements with which Haeckel, as a University Professor of Biology, had no direct involvement. He never entered politics or stood for parliament. (Fascism was not officially inaugurated until 1922, nearly three years after Haeckel's death.)

As for Christians, art was a religious activity but, whereas Christians painted Madonnas, saints and angels, the Monists painted nature, especially the sun, which was not only the giver of life on Earth, it was also pure, unsullied. The 'purity' of the 'yellow' sun in some way enhanced the concept of the 'purity' of the blond, Germanic race. To reproduce an image of nature, be it flower, stream, mountain or stars, one had first to become 'one' with the object one was painting, to 'feel' it, to become immersed with it. This was a religious experience, a form of worship. Painting was not an occupation for the privileged few, who had been born with a natural ability to paint. It was an occupation to be undertaken by all, since it was the act of painting, not the final result, which was uplifting to the spirit. The purpose of Gasman's book was to show how Hitler adopted and adapted Haeckel's idea of Monism into his idea of Nazism, with the Hindu symbol for the sun as its emblem. It will be remembered that, in his earlier years, Hitler strove to be an artist. Now we know why!

Haeckel was not alone in supposing that a person's position in society was the natural outcome of their ability. One found one's own level. The aristocrats tacitly accepted the fact that they had been born to positions of wealth and power due to the endeavours of their ancestors, of which they were proud, but they were not so ready to acknowledge that a member of the lower (working) class had been born to his position of poverty through no 'fault' of his own but due to the position held by his ancestors, which position might, and usually did, stretch back for centuries. That a working person would have the ability to hold a responsible position in the upper echelons of society, given the opportunity (and education) was not considered. It was the aim of the socialist movement to ensure that each individual was afforded equal opportunity to make the most of their abilities, according to their own effort. Haeckel's Monism fitted within this general socialistic framework but with the added component of 'Nature' and Man's place within it, something with which other socialists were not concerned. Equal opportunity – yes, but equal ability? No! The essence of Nature was diversity, inequality, and this, too, must be recognised, even to the extent of disregarding, or even disposing of, those of no use. Haeckel's doctrine, therefore, held a measure of appeal for those who had previously aligned themselves with either the liberal or the socialist position. There was something of each for each.

Monists recognised that people had different levels of ability, both physical and intellectual. Allowing every man an equal voting power would inevitably result in the election to positions of authority those to whom the majority related – i.e., those with mediocre intellectual abilities. This would result in a mediocre society.

While the edict that work should be compulsory for all may have sounded very fair, it failed to take into account increasing mechanisation, which was replacing manual labour with machine labour at an alarming rate – alarming, that is, for the labourers, not for the business owners, nor their customers, who were able to purchase a larger range of goods at prices far lower than would ever have been imagined a century or so previously. I am not aware of any industrialised society today which has solved the problem of unemployment. An unemployment rate of 5% is generally considered 'as good as can be expected' – but that means one in twenty persons out of work. Unemployment numbers do not (usually) include those on sickness or disability benefits. They refer only to people actively seeking work. The sight of an upper class, or aristocratic, person working may bring pleasure to some, but not, I fear, to the poor(er) person, whose job they have taken. Our reaction will be guided either by science (head) or feeling (heart). Which wins out will be a matter of perception!

Haeckel adamantly denied the accusation that he was a socialist and there can be no doubt that he rejected Marx' version of socialism – that of the equality of all people. No two people were born the same. All had differences and some of those difference lifted them in society, others did not. This was true of individuals; this was true of races; this was true of nations. This was Darwinism. But there is more than one thread from which the doctrine of socialism is woven and a second, extremely important thread, is the doctrine of State ownership: State ownership of assets, State ownership of people. It was this aspect of his teaching which has brought Haeckel into consideration within the scope of this study.

The Fascism of Mussolini and the Nazism of Hitler culminated in the outbreak of World War II in August, 1939, twenty years *after* the death of Haeckel, which had occurred on 9th August, 1919.

Gasman's excellent work in bringing to the notice of the English speaking world the ideas of Haeckel and his followers, of the origin and influence of the concept of 'Monism', which became a religion, were undertaken in an attempt to understand the origins of Hitler's Nazi philosophy and its consequence, World War II. Gasman was working backwards, from the result to its beginnings, trying to uncover the roots in order to understand the growth. This work has been undertaken from the opposite perspective. In studying each person, each reformer, I have tried to put out of my mind the future. I have tried to understand that person in the context of his (it was always male) times, his upbringing, his thoughts, his hopes and fears for the future. I am not considering any politicians, who have sought to bring about reform through the passing of Laws. I am considering only reformers who have worked from positions within society.

Haeckel sought the overthrow of the social system, government, as it existed during his lifetime. He sought to replace it with another system, another belief – *his* system, *his* belief. He did not seek to bring freedom of thought or action to others. He sought to bring them into compliance with *his* ideas – purely for their benefit, of course! A pattern is emerging!

14
Love Life

During his lifetime, Bertrand Russell (1872-1970) was the best known of all the persons considered in this book – both his person and his ideas. By the time he started writing, even working class men were reading a daily paper. Although Russell supported equal rights for women, he expended less energy in this cause than he did in many others and he was in his fifties before Universal Suffrage finally became a reality in Britain. His work was aimed at the male leaders of industry and the male politicians and he relied upon the voting male for support. That is not to say that he disregarded the ideas of women – far from it. He was fortunate enough upon several occasions to fall in love with the most beautiful, most loving and most intelligent woman on the face of the Earth, who not only reciprocated his love, but shared his ideas. There were four such women in Russell's life and there is no doubt that, without their support, Russell would never have achieved as much he did.

Russell lived during one of the most fascinating and exciting times in history – from the horse and cart to the bicycle, the car, the plane, the space ship, to man landing on the Moon - Russell experienced it all, if not in person, then by media, which now included, not only radio and film, but television as well! He also experienced two World Wars and the dropping of atomic bombs on Hiroshima and Nagasaki. These events affected him deeply. Russell was an emotional man – bi-polar, manic-depressive, whatever term you wish to use. Russell expended incredible amounts of energy upon the projects in which he became interested and then, by his own account, suffered deep depression when his efforts did not bring about the desired result. Russell does not appear to have been 'up one minute, down the next'. Rather his periods of excitement lasted for months, as did his times of depression. The depressions were the cause of the breakdown of his first three relationships. His moods did seem to stabilise in his old age – he died at the age of ninety-eight.

Understandably, a number of books have been written about Russell but for the purpose of this short account, I have limited myself to his 'Autobiography' and a (substantial) collection of papers and extracts from his works: *The Basic Writings of Bertrand Russell,* which was published in 1961, when Russell was eighty-nine years old. It was compiled by two of his friends, Robert Egner and Lester Donnon, who realised that the up-coming generation would not plough through the heavy tomes which had engaged the Victorian and Edwardian reader, who had been happy to know that the book upon which they were then starting would last them for a couple of weeks – or more! Radio, cinema, television – the young had other things to do, yet much of that which Russell had written was still relevant in the 1960s – and is still relevant today. Much is not, but Egner and Donnon considered it essential for the reader to appreciate the growth of Russell's thinking, the path along which his ideas had travelled. I read the entire book – and I did understand bits and pieces, here and there. I would have understood more if Russell had not been writing about mathematics, science, economics, etc., subjects about which I know next to nothing. I fared better when he was writing about psychology and education. Russell made no contribution to the collation, but he did 'approve' the work, which was published under his name.

For the most part, the following is drawn from Russell's 'Autobiography', although it needs to be stressed that the book was not written by Russell himself, but compiled by a small group of his friends and admirers. Their sources of information were letters kept by Russell or borrowed from recipients of letters Russell had written and chats with surviving family and friends. The book was read and approved by Russell in the last years of his life. The first volume was published in 1967, when Russell was ninety-five years of age, the third in 1970, just before he died at the age of ninety-eight.

According to the *Introduction*, written by Michael Foot, who was, at that time, England's best known Socialist Member of Parliament, Russell took great care to write in plain English, not simply because it was easy to understand but, more importantly, because it was harder to misrepresent. This was an understanding which came to Russell through experience. In his youth, he endeavoured to impress by deliberately writing works which virtually nobody could understand, works on his favourite subject: mathematics. A work on mathematics which could be understood by 'everyone' was not worth writing. All had been said before, When his great work was finally published after years of effort (when he was thirty-eight), he believed that it was understood by but three or four people. He was *delighted*. This number was large enough to prove his work was valid and small enough to show that it was so advanced that it was at the 'cutting edge' of human understanding. Fortunately, he had inherited sufficient money to pay himself the printing cost of this small 'run'.

My copy of the *Autobiography* is a paperback compilation of all three volumes, issued in 2009 by The Bertrand Russel Peace Foundation. Nowhere could I find the names of the friends who 'assisted' Russell in this undertaking. They remained anonymous. This was Russell's Autobiography.

Bertrand became an orphan. He was born 18th May, 1872, when both his parents were thirty years of age. His mother and sister died of diphtheria sometime during 1874 when he was two years old, and his father, Lord Amberley (a former British Prime Minister) died in 1876 from bronchitis, after a period of 'gradually increasing debility'. It must have been very early that year, because in February, 1876, Bertrand arrived at Pembroke

Lodge, the home of his grandfather and grandmother. He was accompanied by his brother, seven years his senior. It was a lonely childhood. Seven years is a big age-gap at that time of life. The only regular play-mate Bertrand had was the son of one of the staff, who was about the same age. When his grandfather died, his brother became Earl. Both were tutored during their Primary school years, but attended Senior school, which was the first opportunity Bertrand had of making friends of his own choosing.

His grandmother was somewhat younger (twenty-three years) than his grandfather. It was she who stood *in locum parentis* after his grandfather died. She doted on him, but, like many teens and twenties young people, Bertrand had little time for her in her twilight years. He was discovering the world. By reading their letters and diaries, Bertrand later learned that both of his parents had been free thinkers, advocating social reform: votes for women and birth control. His grandmother was not a free thinker – far from it - so here 'Nature' definitely won out over 'Nurture'. His grandmother was raised Scotch Presbyterian but later became Unitarian. His grandfather had been Anglican and this was still the predominant faith of the household. Growing up, Bertrand attended Sunday services of different denominations. Not surprisingly, as a teenager, he became somewhat confused. Unfortunately, his grandmother discouraged any discussion relating to religion or philosophy. The lonely child read countless books available to him in their library, pondering over the works of John Stuart Mill (a family friend), Neitsche, many others, both philosophers and poets. He thought much, but had no one with whom to share his ponderings. He became introspective.

It must not be thought that Pembroke Lodge was an empty establishment. At the time Bertrand joined the household, his grandmother had four surviving brothers and two surviving sisters, all of whom would visit from time to time. He mentions some by name – and title: Lord Minto, Sir Henry Elliot, Lady Elizabeth Romilly, Lady Charlotte Portal, Presumably, his grandmother had been a 'Lady' before she married into the

Russell family? Two of his grandmother's unmarried siblings, Uncle Rollo and Aunt Agatha, were permanent residents at Pembroke, Aunt Agatha being only nineteen years older than Bertrand. They may not have been playmates, but Uncle Rollo talked to Russell about 'scientific matters'. He was a meteorologist, taking readings for the Meteriological Office, and those conversations were of great importance to them both. Unmarried, Bertrand records that Uncle Rollo suffered from a morbid shyness which prevented him from mixing with strangers – a condition today known as 'Social Anxiety Disorder'. Conspicuously missing is any mention by Russell of a relative whom he considered completely 'normal'. Of most interest I found the fact that he never gave the name of his brother anywhere in his book. He was always referred to as 'my brother'. They were never close but the giving of a name is a common courtesy. Why this obfuscation? From the *Index* I learned that his brother's name was Francis (Frank).

As already mentioned, Bertrand's grandfather was a former Prime Minister of the United Kingsom and Pembroke Lodge had been gifted to him by Queen Victoria in recognition of his service to the Country. Russell described it as a rambling house of only two storeys, set in eleven acres of land, most of which was allowed to run wild. (This was usual practice.) It was part of Richmond Park, with views across Epsom Downs to Windsor Castle.

Cold baths, no fruit. That was the medical advice of the day in regard to the rearing of children. His affluent/orphan status made no difference in this respect. Materially, he was far 'better off' than the children being raised in the Victorian slums, but they had something which he did not – companionship. He would have traded a walk in the park for hop-scotch in the street any day!

Russell records that during his teenage years, three subjects consumed his mind: sex, religion and mathematics. His mind continued to be obsessed with sex throughout his life. Religion? If one was right, the others must be wrong. But which? After much reading and even more thought, Russell concluded that *all* religions were wrong. For a while, he struggled with the 'First Cause' argument but eventually decided that it did not provide an answer, merely pushed the question one stage further back. He became an ardent atheist. Later, his position softened. He became agnostic. It was not so much the beauty of the Earth which entranced him, but the beauty of the skies, which he had plenty of opportunity to observe from his country retreats. He never attributed personal characteristics, such as love, to any primeval or cosmic force.

That left mathematics – the one certainty in his world upon which he felt he could rely. Russell was a highly intelligent man, a deep thinker who, when he had embraced a topic, endeavoured to follow it through to the end, however long that might take. At the age of eleven, he was introduced to Euclid. From then, until the age of thirty-eight, when his book was finally published, mathematics was his chief source of happiness. During his adolescence he came to believe that the achievement of happiness was the primary aim of life – both for the individual and for societies, as collections of individuals. Everyone was entitled to seek their own happiness but their own happiness could only be achieved if they perceived happiness in those around them.

During his childhood, Russell had no personal understanding of the difficulties experienced by those living in the Victorian slums, or even those employed, earning an income sufficient to support their family, but only by dint of hard work over many hours. These understandings came to him in his adult years. For the rest of his life, Russell expressed deep sympathy and concern for the poor, the downtrodden. Unfortunately, Russell was a man of ideas, but not of much practicality. Unlike Owen, there was no one in Russell's immediate circle in need of his assistance. The servants at Pembroke Lodge were well cared for and lived in a luxurious environment. His understanding of advanced mathematics was of no help. Whether managing the household budget or the nation's budget, economics required but basic mathematical skills. But Bertrand had one more skill – a skill by no means unique to him but one in which he excelled.

Words! He could write – letters to the Editor, articles for newspapers, journals. He could write books. As his skill grew, his readership grew, his influence grew.

The word 'compulsive' is often associated with 'obsessive' and obsessive compulsive people are frequently hoarders. Russell did not hoard objects but he did hoard knowledge – and words! It is said that he never forgot a word he read (photographic memory?). He wrote to convey knowledge (initially) but his biographers said that he took delight in the composition of his sentences, as much for their vocabulary and their syntax, as for their meaning, which he endeavoured to express in a manner both simple and clear. As a teenager, he had sought to elevate himself above other people; in his old age, he sought rather to mix with the common crowd, albeit as a 'leader' rather than as a 'follower'.

In 1890, at the age of eighteen, Russell left home to experience Cambridge – the University, that is. He quickly made friends with a fellow student, whom he refers to only as 'Sanger'. It was a friendship which was to last a lifetime, Sanger's lifetime, that is. He died in 1930. Students form groups, clubs, societies. One such at Cambridge was known simply as 'The Society' and Russell was invited to join this elect group in his second year, 1892. Members met every Saturday night and no subject was barred.

Russell's obtuse work on mathematics was his pride and joy, the great accomplishment of his life during its first one-third, while he was associating with the University crowd, under- and post-graduate. As he started to travel, visiting, holidaying, he became aware of the difficulties faced by others. As already discussed when considering Owen, industrialisation was a two-edged sword. It brought many advantages, but those advantages were not evenly shared across the population – hence the rise of socialism. Russell became a socialist. Russell mentioned the name of Henry George as being instrumental in arousing his interest in land nationalisation. He made no mention of Wallace, although this was the time during which Wallace established his Land Nationalisation Association, writing very extensively upon the subject, offering specific solutions and a time-line for their implementation.

Russell joined the Labour Party and three times was persuaded to stand for Parliament. Three times he failed to be elected, but that does not mean that he was not a good candidate. On each occasion, he had been pressured into nominating for a seat, held by the Conservatives, which the Labour Party had expectations of winning – with the right candidate – which they hoped would be the well-known, articulate Bertrand Russell. That was not to be, which was probably a good thing for all concerned. I have tried to imagine Russell attending sittings when required, standing when told to stand, sitting when told to sit, speaking only when the Speaker gave him permission to speak and then only uttering words his superiors had given him permission to utter. Promoting other peoples' visions – No! Russell was a rebel, not a slave!

Russell's embracing of socialism took time. During his teens and twenties, Russell had been consumed by his interest in mathematics (certainty) and religious philosophy (uncertainty). It was not until after he completed his University studies, when he started to travel, at home and abroad, that Russell began to see the real world and what it had to offer, both good and bad. His Grandmother became concerned by his lack of direction. It was not considered appropriate in those times for a wealthy person to undertake paid work if that meant a job being taken away from some other person who needed the wage to feed his family but that did not mean that the wealthy were idle. They undertook vast amounts of voluntary work, especially in relation to hospitals. Russell, at that time, was contributing nothing to society. He was just amusing himself. His grandmother arranged for him to undertake a three months' assignment as a relief diplomat at the Embassy in Paris, hoping this would lead to a career in the Diplomatic Service. Russell completed the three months – and came back home. That was the only paid employment he undertook throughout his entire life. Nevertheless, the time was well spent. It determined in Russell's mind what he did *not* want to do – answer to anybody else! He determined to support himself by writing. His early books on mathematics and philosophy were too obtuse to attract many purchasers. He paid for their publication himself, out of his small inheritance. With time, he learned to write books on subjects in which people were interested, in language which they could understand. He became one of England's most successful writers.

Bertrand's first marriage took place on 13th December, 1894. His bride was Alys Smith, a Quaker, five years his senior. By mutual agreement, the marriage remained childless. Living in the country, with no children to distract him, Russell was able to concentrate on his writing. In 1895, he went to Germany to study German Social Democracy, about which he lectured on his return at The London School of Economics, which had recently been established. In 1896, he published his first book on socialism. Germany was not his only interest; indeed, it was not his main one. Every year, from his marriage until the outbreak of war in 1914, he and Alys visited Italy – twenty years in all. In the autumn of 1898, he and Alys spent three months in America, Alys' family being residents of Chicago.

Russell records writing the last words of *The Principles of Mathematics* on 31st December, 1899, the last day of the century. Its completion may have brought a moment of temporary triumph but that moment was followed by a time of deep depression: "the darkest despair I have ever known" (p.136).

In 1901, he, and his childhood friend, Whitehead (with their respective wives) jointly moved into the house of a mutual friend, who was moving overseas for a time. Mrs. Whitehead was increasingly suffering pain from a weak heart. He and Alys arrived home one evening to find Mrs. Whitehead engulfed in agony, This was a turning point in Russell's life. Russell was suddenly overwhelmed with an understanding of the supreme loneliness of each human soul in its agony (p.137):

> ... the loneliness of the human soul is unendurable; nothing can penetrate it except the highest intensity of love that

religious teachers have preached, whatever does not spring from this motive is harmful, or at best useless; it follows that war is wrong, that a public school education is abominable, that the use of force is to be deprecated, and that in human relations one should penetrate to the core of loneliness in each person and speak to that.

At the end of those five minutes, he recalls, he had become a completely different person, no longer caring about the exactness and analysis of the material world. From now on he was filled with a desire to find a 'philosophy' which would make human life endurable. This feeling, that every other human being was suffering from the same feelings of loneliness that he was feeling at that point in time, never left him, although it does seem to have moderated in his final years. His own times of loneliness and depression were interspersed with times of great joy and happiness but, for some reason, he never transferred those feelings, in his mind, to the rest of humanity.

Although Russell always spoke of *Principia Mathematica* as though it was his book, alone, in fact it was written with the collaboration of his good friend, Whitehead. I have no doubt that the original mathematical thought was Russell's; Whitehead would have enacted more the role of editor. Volume I was published In 1910, volume II in 1912 and volume III in 1913. Sales were low; he lost money as the result of his years of work. He stated that his intellect never recovered from the strain and that that was the reason why there was a change in the nature of his work. The following year he was made a Fellow of the Royal Society, a coveted honour.

Being a supporter of Free Trade, in 1910 Russell offered himself for pre-selection as a candidate for the Liberal Party, but was rejected because of his agnostic views. Still a supporter, he resolved to help a neighbouring candidate, Philip Morrell, a friend of his brother-in-law, who was married to Lady Ottoline Cavendish-Bentinck. Philip was called away for the night and he was left 'tête-a-tête' with Ottoline, with whom he fell deeply in love that same evening. Ottoline had no desire to be divorced. Such an act would not only have deprived her of her home, it would have separated her from her children. At that time, the man, being the breadwinner, automatically gained custody of any children. Ottoline and Bertrand simply 'had an affair'. Her husband, Philip, tolerated the situation, but insisted that they should never spend the night together, so Bertrand made sure he left their rendez-vous by midnight. The affair lasted about six years and then petered out.

It was during this time war broke out. For the first time in his life, Russell became personally involved in a 'Cause' – that of pacifism.

In 1914, he was invited to lecture in Boston and, on 7th March, sailed to America aboard the *Mauretania*. He was made a temporary Professor at Harvard where he gave a course of lectures on applying the scientific method to philosophical thinking, before returning home. Being invited to lecture at Harvard was an honour, although Russell found the American University somewhat 'staid' in comparison with the more free-thinking Cambridge.

Before the outbreak of war, Russell's interests had been metaphysical: mathematics, philosophy. The war brought him into touch with reality. Part of that reality surprised him. He had always thought that wars were forced upon a reluctant population by a determined ruler. Not so! Moving around London, speaking to 'average men and women', he was amazed by the support expressed for the war. Even his good friends, the Whiteheads, supported the war. Russell was forced to reconsider his whole concept of human nature. He had supposed that most parents loved their children, but now he witnessed parents encouraging their sons to risk injury/death by volunteering to fight. He found that many (politicians?) preferred popularity over truth. Russell, himself, was torn between his love of England and his hatred of war (p.227):

> ... when the war came, I felt I heard the voice of God. I knew that it was my business to protest.

Being too old to be conscripted, Russell was spared the horrors of active duty on 'The Front' but the news, via radio and print, kept everybody informed in a way which had never happened before. In former times, soldiers 'went off to War', returned to tell their tales of horror or to hold their silence, according to their nature, but for the people left behind, it was a story, almost a fairy tale: George and the Dragon. Not so, this time. No German soldier set foot on British soil but that was not to say that Britain was not under attack. We hear much about the Blitz, the German air-raids of World War II but little of the German Air Raids of World War I. But they happened! The planes were smaller; they carried smaller loads of smaller bombs but they came. The pilots tried to drop their bombs where they would destroy some infrastructure of importance, a railway, a factory, but it was impossible to aim with accuracy and civilians (of all ages) were injured or killed.

Russell became [a] leader of the No Conscription Fellowship. Through this Fellowship, he met up with a young lady by the name of Collette O'Neil. She was married to Miles Malleson, an actor and playwright. and she, herself was an actress. He walked her home one night and they became lovers, although they scarcely knew each other. At a Christmas party, Keynes read the marriage service over two dogs (the two required witnesses?) and ended "Whom man hath joined, let not dog put asunder".

In 1916, Russell wrote another leaflet for the Fellowship; those who distributed it were sent to prison. That was hardly fair – on Russell. He wrote a letter to *The Times* and was 'rewarded' with a fine of €100 – not an inconsiderable amount. Of course, he refused to pay and some of his belongings were sold to raise the amount. These were bought by friends, who returned the items to him, which, he wrote, made his protest 'rather futile'.

He fared better with his next effort. In an article published in *The Tribunal* in early 1918, he suggested that American troops stationed in England would be used as 'strike breakers'. This earned him a six months' gaol sentence. Political influence ensured that he was placed in first division. His cell was large enough to accommodate a table and typewriter. He was free to write another book, just so long as the subject was not pacifism. It was on mathematics. Ottoline and Collette both visited him, bringing him books he needed for his research, taking back the ones with which he was finished. This enabled him to smuggle letters out of the gaol. Russell left prison September, 1918, when the war was all but over. Collette had fallen in love with someone else. Well. That's life!

The war changed Russell. He was no longer interested in abstract matters but in the trials and tribulations of ordinary humans. Suffering from loneliness and depression himself, he assumed that others were suffering in the same way – albeit trying to hide their distress. It was these indescribable feelings which drove people to despair and war. His mission in life was to bring about change.

15
Worth Fighting For

Russell first met his second wife in 1916, at a dinner. Everybody at the table declared what they most desired in life and Dora (Black) said 'Marriage and children', which was an unexpected response at a dinner party comprised of philosophers. At the time Russell was still involved with Collette but her married status put marriage and children out of reach. Russell was forty-four. He had come to crave children of his own. In 1919, he invited Dora to tea, with a few friends, and the relationship began from there, but slowly, because Russell had other things to occupy him, such as travelling.

In 1920, Russell went to Barcelona and then to Majorca. On returning to England, an opportunity arose for him to visit Russia, as part of a Labour delegation. At that time, the Tsar and his family were still surviving but Lenin was in charge. The country was full of cruelty, poverty, suspicion and persecution. Poor drinking water, poor sanitation, flies, mosquitoes; plague was endemic, sickness was everywhere. Equality was everywhere (except among the elite): same houses, same clothes, same education, same thought – or, at least, the same *expressed* thought. Was there any difference between past and present – except the ruler? Money might not bring happiness, but lack of it did not bring happiness either! He came to feel that all politics was inspired by a 'grinning devil'. He spent an hour with Lenin, but was not impressed with his intellect.

Dora had wanted to accompany him, but he said: 'No'. He expected her to meet him at Stockholm on his return but was surprised to find that she had left Stockholm – to go to Russia! It was an extended visit; Russell received letters from her from which he learned that she loved Russia as much as he had hated it. Russell received an invitation to lecture in China for a year. If Dora was to accompany him, she must return at once. She did. Five days later, they left England for China. He found the Chinese to be the most civilised people in the world. The cold winter weather took its toll. He developed bronchitis, became delirious, was hospitalised, was at death's door and when he recovered, three months later, had lost his memory of all that had happened. He could not even remember his own name. He was nursed in a hospital staffed by German nurses. His main illness had been double pneumonia but he was also diagnosed with heart disease, kidney disease, dysentery and phlebitis. I could not help but feel it a pity that the opportunity had not been taken by him to experience Chinese medicine. Despite that missed opportunity, he recovered well. Early in his convalescence, Dora discovered she was pregnant. Although still very weak, by 10th July he was well enough for them to leave Peking.

Although his planned lecture tour of Japan had to be cancelled, they did spend twelve days there and he did give one lecture. An interesting thing happened as he and Dora arrived at Yokohama. He was greeted by a display of fireworks. This sent him 'blind with rage'. He feared the noise and bright magnesium flashes might cause Dora to miscarry. His weakness prevented him from catching the boys who had lit the fireworks, a good thing, he concluded, because if he had, he would have killed them. Not the sentiment of a pacifist! At that moment, he realised that some things were worth fighting for, killing for, dying for.

They sailed from Yokohama and arrived back in England mid August, were married on 17th September and their first child, John, (Lord Amberley) was born 16th November, 1921. Russell mentioned the birth of a second child but gave no details of date or sex. The couple divided their time between London and Cornwall. He did mention Kate reciting a verse she had made up about the weather one April day when she was two years and three months old. Kate was born in the month of January; because the two children were close in age, I presume the year was 1923. Education became a subject of great interest and Russell wrote a book, published in 1926: *On Education, especially in early Childhood*. This book was written *before* his children commenced their formal education. In 1924, he made another lecture tour of America, presumably without the family? He stood for Parliament in 1922 and 1923, Dora in 1924. Women had but recently been granted the right to vote. Was Dora the first female to stand for the British Parliament? The children were in the care of a nurse and a governess, giving Dora time to pursue her own interests, if she so desired.

By 1927, the time had come for the children to attend school – but there was no school which met their expectations. There was no other option: they must start a school of their own., The couple collected a group of about twenty children, whom they hoped would stay together throughout their school days. This hope, like so many others of Russell's, was dashed. Russell had rented a property owned by his brother, set in two hundred and thirty acres of land. The school ran at a loss. Fortunately, Russell's books were selling well and he made a further three lecture tours of America: 1927, 1929, 1931. Dora, also, made a lecture tour of America. It is unclear quite how many staff were employed – the children needed to be fed. It is unclear quite how much contact the children had with their own parents or whether the overseas lectures took place during the school holidays? I assume they did. Even so, when home Russell spent most of his time writing – to make money to support the school. There was only one teacher for the children. One teacher is enough for a class of twenty; but 'give them a break!' There was yet another problem: problem children! The parents most likely to experiment with the education of their children were the parents of children who had difficulties with the established system. John and Kate were thought by the other children to be favoured by their parents. This caused Bertrand and Dora to take pains *not* to favour them, rather the reverse. The close relationship between Bertrand and Dora and their two children was lost. Happy Days!

It was not only the school which failed. His marriage failed too. After he left Dora, she continued the school for a number of years, although not at the same place after he reclaimed the property. Their two children were made wards in Chancery and sent to Dartington schools 'where they were very happy'.

Having failed as a parent, Russell gave up writing 'pot-boilers' (books on personal relationships, education, etc.) and turned his attention once again to more important matters. Although the Great Depression was officially over, people were more frugal, buying fewer books. Bertrand's financial situation became quite dire. He could no longer afford to pay his brother the rent on the school house, and its two hundred and thirty acres. Dora had to vacate the premises. He moved in, with the intention of refurbishing the place to make it suitable for sale. Having moved in, he went to the Canary Islands for a holiday. On his return, he found himself devoid of inspiration so he wrote a book about the menace of war, continuing his pacifist approach. There was a problem. He hated Hitler; he hated the Nazis. He recognised that he, himself, no longer believed what he was preaching. In the school, Russell had found stern authority necessary if the weaker persons were not be be bullied and oppressed. Somebody (some Body) had to be that authority. He worked on a couple of projects (one a biography of his parents and their reformative ideas) with Patricia (Peter) Spence, whom he married in 1936, when he was sixty-four. His second son, Conrad, was born in 1937. The school house and its two hundred and thirty acres was eventually sold in 1938.

In March, 1931, Russell's brother had died unexpectedly, while in Marseilles. He had no children. Russell inherited the family title, becoming an Earl, but nothing else, except the school house, with its two hundred and thirty acres, which he had already taken over. Perhaps his brother's unexpected early death turned Russell's mind towards the uncertainties of life – after all, both his parent's died young. For whatever reason, mid 1931 Russell wrote a short Autobiography, which formed the basis of the Autobiography collated by his friends in the 1960s. In the *Epilogue*, which was reproduced, with Britain's influence already in decline, he forecast the future domination of the world by either America or Russia. In either case, he foresaw tight control exercised by the State over the individual.

In the Autumn of 1938, John and Kate returned to Dartington; he, Peter and Conrad sailed for America, where Russell became a Professor at the University of California. In August, 1939, John and Kate came to visit, a visit which was intended to coincide with the school holidays but turned out coinciding with the outbreak of war. They were stuck. It wasn't that Hitler *wanted* to waste precious torpedoes sinking passenger ships. He wanted to sink ships bringing much needed supplies to Britain. Nevertheless, a mistake *might* be made. No passenger ships crossed the Atlantic for more than four years. The family finally sailed home May, 1944.

On his return, Russell was offered a five year position lecturing once again at Cambridge. In 1949, his marriage came to an end.

Something else had ended – the war. In May, 1945, the war in Europe ground to a halt. Hitler was no more. We did not hate the German people for what they had done to us. We sympathised with them for what Hitler had done to them. There was no talk of reparation, only of co-operation. The war with Japan dragged on, but Japan had never been a threat to Britain. It was with the South-East (Malaysia, Philippines, New Guinea, Australia) that Japanese interest lay. Many of these places had strong affiliation with European countries, particularly Britain and Holland. At the beginning of August, that war came to an abrupt end with the dropping of two atomic bombs, one on Hiroshima, one on Nagasaki. At seventy-three years of age, Russell had learned enough about human behaviour no longer to embrace pacifism in all its forms, but 'pacifism' in the form of 'non-nuclear' became the Cause which dominated the final twenty-five years of his life.

Russell was not the only person to feel that way. His feelings were shared by millions of people, not only in Britain, not only in Europe, but throughout the world. Russell's social position (as an English Earl), his non-political position, not being a Member of Parliament, nor a Diplomat of any description, as well as his status as one of Britain's best known writers, set him apart from all other activists. He met and/or corresponded with eminent people, both at home and abroad. The *rapprochement* between East and West which followed the death of Stalin in 1953 enabled face-to-face talks to be held at regular intervals between America and Russia, which always resulted in agreements to destroy and dispose of a certain number of nuclear weapons from their respective arsenal. Agreements were sealed with a hand shake and a smile, but we all knew that the weapons to be destroyed were obsolete as more and more nuclear testing took place, at first above ground, then below, but never unnoticed. The seismic waves were registered by equipment designed to detect earth tremors/quakes. The hydrogen bomb joined the arsenal. Throughout the sixties, Russell continued to preach his doctrine of fear: fear that a nuclear war was 'inevitable', almost certainly before the end of the decade, unless a radical change could be brought about in the attitudes of those who ruled the world.

Supporting, as he did, the concept of a World Government, which would take equal care of the interests of every individual member country, Russell welcomed both NATO (North Atlantic Treaty Organisation) and the United Nations. He envisaged the members of the United Nations working in concert, not forming cliches to enhance the position of one group of countries against another – in other words, not acting like a Parliament! During Russell's life-time, the United Nations' peace-keeping force, known as the 'Blue Berets', unarmed, kept protagonists apart. The British Police at that time were unarmed. It was against the criminal code of honour to shoot an unarmed policeman and it was against the rebel code of honour to shoot an unarmed Peacekeeper – until the 1970s, when somebody did.

During this time, Russell was full of despair, which he described as a feeling of impending doom, such as some people experience as the clouds gather before the outbreak of a thunder storm. For him, the feared lightening strike was the nuclear blast.

No longer pacifist, but still anti-aggression, Russell's speeches were welcomed by the authorities to the extent that in 1949 he was awarded the Order of Merit (OM), which delighted him. His socialism was directed against the industrialist millionaire, rising to richness on the shoulders of the down-trodden poor; he never wrote against the Monarchy,

In 1950, he was invited by the Labour Government to visit Australia. He went to every State, except Tasmania, particularly enjoying his visit to Alice Springs. He gave many speeches, but the exact purpose of his visit remains unclear. His next stop was America, once again. There he renewed acquaintance with Einstein and received news that he was to be awarded a Nobel Prize for literature. The year 1950, starting with the OM and ending with the Nobel Prize, marked the epitome of Russell's 'respectability'.

I was about to say that, for the rest of his life, Russell was consumed with one passion, that passion being Nuclear Disarmament, but that is not quite true. He had another passion – his fourth wife. While on a visit to America n 1950, he met with a friend, whose acquaintance he had made on a previous visit about half a century previously. She relocated to London. Although in his Autobiography, Russell gave no date, the *Chronology* at the front of *Basic Writings* showed 1952 as being the year in which he divorced Patricia (Peter) and married Edith Finch. It was the year in which he turned seventy; it was to be his final marriage.

The couple embarked upon an extended honeymoon: France, Italy, Greece. Russell had never been to Greece before and was much taken by it. 1953 was the turn of Scotland. While there, he developed a severe sore throat, which was thought to be cancer. Happily not – and the cause was never determined, although his throat continued to be troublesome. I suspect something which in my days as a therapist was known as 'Speaker's Throat' – i.e. talking too much! During that time he learned of the illness of his eldest son, John. The cause of the illness is never identified, but it was serious and ongoing. Being a teenager at that time, I remember the most feared disease and am going to hazard a guess his son had developed leukaemia. Leukaemia usually developed in the teens/twenties, affecting more boys than girls, although nobody seemed to know why. It was incurable. As the body lost its ability to replace red blood cells, the victim became pale, weak, and finally died. Salvation came, not through medicine, but through surgery – bone marrow transplants.

Russell records that his son, wife and three children were living in a tiny house, far too small for their family but, unfortunately, Russell did not have enough money to help him into a larger place of his own. Instead, Russell and Edith moved into a larger place, his son and family occupying the lower two floors, and Russel and Edith the upper two. Christmas, 1953, his son and his wife decided they were 'tired of children', left the table after Christmas dinner, taking the left-over food with them, but not the children, who, thereafter, remained in the care of Bertrand and Edith (or the staff they employed). This was a further financial burden upon Bertrand, who felt he was already carrying quite enough burdens in the form of alimony payments. Russell made John sound quite selfish, but if I am right that John was suffering from a serious illness, such as leukaemia, then it is not only possible, but quite likely, that John was physically incapable of caring for his children. His wife's energies would have been taken up with caring for him.

As Russell's fame was growing, and he was now in possession of a well-respected title, Russell was able to make 'high level' approaches to world leaders, discussions either held in person, by telephone or by letter. His 'unofficial' status, neither parliamentarian nor diplomat, gave him a freedom not enjoyed by others. He travelled extensively around his home country, speaking, not merely to such officials as were polite enough to listen, but to the people. He felt the need to find some way to make the world understand the dangers its was facing: "into which it was running blindly". l am not quite sure why he thought he was the only person with this awareness, why he felt the Presidents of Russia and America to be so naive. The Cuban crisis (1962) came and went. Russell travelled, at home and abroad; he spoke to powerful individuals, to powerless crowds, in person and by radio; he published, letters, articles, in newspapers, journals, his own publications. He did anything and everything he could and he continued to do this, with the help of his wife, until his dying day.

In July, 1960, Russell received a visit from a young American by the name of Ralph Schoeman, who was very keen to incorporate civil disobedience within the anti-nuclear movement. The Committee for Nuclear Disarmament (CND) already involved a Direct Action Committee, but its activities were strictly legal. Russell was taken with the idea of Civil Disobedience which found no favour among his colleagues. Eventually, he resigned from the CND, preferring to work with Schoeman. This happened on 5th November, 1960: Guy Forkes' Day. Was he sending a message – or was this just coincidental? The new civil disobedience movement came to be known as the Committee of 100. The primary act of civil disobedience was the 'sit-down'. Of course, the 'sit-downs' were not in parks or in the countryside. They were in places such as Trafalgar Square, where they impeded others' free passage. Pictures (on the increasingly available television) of police (usually more than one officer) dragging away a non-resistant person presented a damaging image of the Police Force, even though they were but doing their duty. Police brutality. Perfect! These marches attracted thousands of participants; Russell became concerned that they had begun to take on the atmosphere of a Sunday picnic.

A large protest was planned for 6th August, 'Hiroshima Day'. The protest began in Hyde Park; where else? Hyde Park was home to 'Speakers' Corner', where anybody might stand on a soap box and proclaim their message, whatever it might be.

Nothing was forbidden – except direct treason. Urging the downfall of the monarch was allowed; urging the killing of the monarch was not. Since there was always a number of Speakers striving to be heard (in my childhood I observed them, as I lived close by) and since the Park was a place of public recreation, microphones were prohibited. Russell started his address with the use of a microphone. A policeman quietly asked him to desist. He refused. The microphone was then forcibly removed by the police officer – to Russell's eye a really 'good look': a young police officer wresting a microphone from the hands of a somewhat frail eighty-eight year old man. This was the signal for the protesters to march down Oxford Street to Trafalgar Square. Russell records a thunderstorm 'of majestic proportions' which broke over them as they were making their march, which was followed by a 'sit down', obstructing access to the Square. More civil disobedience. The end of a perfect day.

Russell and Edith were presented with summons to appear in Court on 12th September, 1960, to answer a charge of inciting civil disobedience. His barrister thought that, in view of Russell's poor health, he would be able to prevent a prison sentence, but that was not what Russell wanted. At Russell's insistence, the barrister presented the defence in such a way that the pair were each sentenced to two months' gaol, commuted to one week, on account of poor health. There were many supporters outside the Court. This angered Russell who knew they meant well, but he wished they would keep quiet. He was deliberately incurring the punishment and did not want the Judge swayed towards compassion.

Large as was the support he received for his anti-nuclear campaign, support was by no means universal. Russell was surprised by the resigned acceptance of many to the possibility (inevitability?) of future war, future use of weapons of mass destruction. He came to understand that there was another emotion in men, stronger than that of self-preservation, and that was the 'desire to get the better of the other fellow'. It was this desire which caused men to enlist, despite the obvious risk to their health and welfare, even to their life. Defence was good; attack was even better. Indeed, the ability to attack was the best defence.

Russell's separation from the CND movement turned out to be very fortuitous. He was free to form other connections. All across the globe, Europe, Asia, America, Africa, there were people wrongfully imprisoned – or, at least, wrongfully imprisoned in the eyes of Russell and his colleagues. They campaigned, often successfully, for their release. Gradually, their loose association and co-operation became sufficiently formalised that on 29th September, 1963, The Bertrand Russell Peace Foundation was formed. He insists that he opposed the Foundation carrying his name, but was over-ruled. In the last ten years of his life, Russell was associated with a group of people who actually achieved what they set out to achieve, at least on some occasions, and that achievement was praiseworthy.

Russell had been born a 'Rebel without a Cause'. He rebelled against the authority of his carers, his older relations, then his tutors, anyone with any authority over him. As he became an adult with no one in direct authority over him, he transferred his attention to Church and State. Although he came to realise that there were some wars that had to be fought, there is no doubt that Russell was, at heart, a gentle person. He sought no violent Revolution. However, he did seek authority. Always, he tried to disguise this desire beneath the cloak of concern, concern for the welfare of others, but it is clear that he considered this 'welfare' would only eventuate when the world operated in the way that he thought it should. He was not as lazy as Spencer, who spent most of his life (when not strolling in somebody else' well-cared for garden) sitting in a chair, either reading or dictating. His travels were continual and extensive. He utilised the printed word, but only along side the spoken word. Even as his health failed him, following a heart attack in his seventies, his enthusiasm gave his body the strength and energy to carry on. He is a man to be admired, as were Owen and Wallace, but in his desire for authority, he out-striped those we have considered before him. He has earned his place in this book on *The Secret Self of Socialism* because, deep below the surface, lay an unrealised desire – the desire that the perfect world operate in accordance with his vision, his desire, his Will.

16
Totalitarianism

And so, we come, at last, to George Orwell, the name irrevocably associated with the authorship of two novels: *Animal Farm* and *Nineteen Eighty-Four*. Published in 1948, *Nineteen Eighty-Four* was written with the clear purpose of alerting the people of post-war Britain to the evils being perpetrated by the Stalinist regime upon the people of Russia.

At that time, Britain herself was suffering under the most totalitarian regime it had suffered since the time of Oliver Cromwell. No sooner had the war ended than the War-time Coalition Government was declared 'over' and a new election was called. Winston Churchill and his Conservative Party were ill-prepared for a campaign. Not so Clement Attlee and his Labour Party, which swept to power. Attlee set about 'Nationalising' services, such as the railways, electricity, telephone, taking over (with little, or no, compensation, I believe) private enterprises, into which certain people had invested immense amounts of time and money. He also commenced the nationalisation of housing. Any new house built automatically belonged to the government. This led to many bomb-damaged houses being repaired, rather than replaced. All leases currently in place became indefinite. No tenant could be evicted, even after their lease had expired. If they failed to pay the rent the matter could be taken to Court, at great time, trouble and expense, and the chance of the landlord recovering any back-payments was slim. All rents remained fixed, indefinitely. Income tax on 'unearned income' (rents and investments) was €1. 0s. 6d. In the pound. In other words, landlords received no rent; they lost six pence for every pound they didn't receive!

Bread was never rationed during the war, but it was after! All food was more severely rationed after the war than during, especially eggs. We were used to dried egg powder for cooking but fresh eggs had been available for meal times. At one time after the war, the ration fell as low as one egg per person, per month! There were four of us in our family; my father had a boiled egg for breakfast each Sunday. My mother served it; my sister and I watched him eat it.

Rationing finally ended in 1952. Orwell had died of tuberculosis in January 1950. It was during the very dark post-War years than Orwell wrote his best-known book, Nineteen Eighty-Four, which was published in 1948. I feel it is important to understand the circumstances prevailing at the time of the book's writing. The common people were aware that things were tough in Russia under Stalin, but they had their own problems to worry about. Orwell was happy inasmuch as he was an ardent supporter of Attlee's socialist government. Attlee's socialist government was happy; they supported Stalin – Orwell did not. What confusion!

It must be remembered that, during the war, Russia was Britain's strongest ally. We tend to think of 'The Allies' as being Britain, her Empire, and America. America sold Britain weapons, generously allowing her to make delayed payments. (It was after the turn of the millennium that Britain finally settled the last account.) American soldiers took an active part in the fighting when the Allies invaded Normandy. That invasion might never have taken place if it had not been for Russia, which country was the true saviour of Britain. Not that they wanted to be, of course! With the Blitzkrieg of Britain having failed, Hitler decided to invade Russia. Hundreds of thousands of German troops crossed the border, cities were encircled and laid under siege. The Russian winter fell – and so did countless soldiers. Millions starved to death, both inside and outside the city walls. Hitler's military might never recovered. A couple of years later, the Russians moved into Germany from the East; the Allies invaded from the West. And the rest, as they say, is history!

The debt Britain owed Russia was different from the one she owed America and, with the Socialist/Communist Attlee Government directing foreign policy, there was little criticism of Russia and Stalin, but there was one man who saw the truth. That man had just published a very successful book, *Animal Farm*, conceived in the late 1930s, written during the early 1940s and published in 1945. Riding the wave of success, he wrote, he published, he enjoyed the flush of success but died before Attlee lost power, before Stalin died, long before the evil he so stoutly resisted finally crumbled.

Who was this man and why did he so fervently resist authoritarian government?

My edition of *Animal Farm*, published in 1987, contains two *Appendices*, one *Afterword* and *A Note on the Text*. It is from these sources that I have obtained biographical information as well as some thoughts and comments of the writers. *Appendix I* was the *Preface* which Orwell had written for *Animal Farm*. It was quite lengthy (for a *Preface*) and could not be included due to paper restrictions. Paper was rationed during, and after, the War. We re-used envelopes, cutting them open carefully and re-sealing them with a square of pastel-coloured gummed paper. Newspapers were two sheets. Books were restricted in page length – margins were narrower, print was smaller. Orwell had conceived the story of *Animal Farm* in the late 1930s, wrote it in the early 1940s, but was unable to find a publisher – hardly surprising, considering the circumstances. It was finally published in 1945, although paper restrictions continued for several more years; the original *Preface* had to be omitted.

Appendix II was Orwell's *Preface* to a special edition published in the Ukrainian language for Ukrainian people living in Germany after the war, in camps for Displaced Persons. In this

Preface, Orwell tells his reader about himself, his life, his thoughts and ideas, his reason for writing. The *Afterword* is a twenty-four page long commentary by Robert Colls and the *Note on the Text*, a short contribution by Peter Davison, these two persons being responsible for the new edition.

The following information has been gleaned from these sources.

'George Orwell' was the pen-name of Eric Arthur Blair, who was born in India in 1903, his father being a Civil Servant attached to the Embassy. At what level was not said, merely that he was an 'official in English Administration', but all British Embassy staff would have been comfortably housed and well fed. There is no reason to believe that the first few years of Eric's life would not have been happy. The precise time of the family's return to England was not stated, nor the reason, but after his return Eric attended a 'Prep' (Preparatory) school before winning a scholarship to Eton.

In his *Preface* to the Ukranian edition of *Animal Farm*, Blair described his family as 'ordinary middle class'. I doubt that. I suspect that Blair was trying to connect with his readers, who were in a German camp for Displaced Persons. It is doubtful that many of them would even have heard of Eton, but those that had would know that it was England's most prestigious school. Few 'ordinary middle class' families would enrol their boys in expensive 'Preparatory' schools – schools designed to prepare students for elite education. Still fewer would have entered their sons to sit for a scholarship to Eton! I accept his claim that had he not won the scholarship, his father would not have been able to afford to pay the fees for Eton, but I suspect that he would have been enrolled at a lesser Public School or a Grammar School. The evidence suggests to me that the Blair family was Upper Middle Class, at least, possibly Lower Upper Class.

I am dwelling upon this matter for two reasons. Firstly, his early (affluent) years contrasted very strongly with some of his later years and this contrast had a profound effect upon his views, indeed was the driving force behind the writing of his two most famous books. The second is that Blair really should have known better! Was he not criticising those in positions of power/authority for disseminating misleading information? Playing down some facts, enhancing/emphasising others, for political/personal gain? Was that not the behaviour in which totalitarian regimes excelled in order to keep the 'proles' (proletariat) compliant? Was that which Blair was doing, trying to down-play his Upper Class childhood, not a similar 'misrepresentation' designed to draw others 'on side'?

Kindergarten-aged children accept as play-mates any child near them in the group. 'Friends' change from day-to-day. Primary school-age children form longer-term friendships. If Eric had achieved double digits by the time he left India, he would have left friends behind. Friends he made at 'Prep' school may not have accompanied him to Eton, which school he would have entered at around 13-14 years of age (male puberty). Eton was a boarding school. During term time, he would have been separated from his parents. Even with the most loving parents in the world, it is inevitable that he experienced times of loneliness, bewilderment, and this at the time of life when human character and emotions are at their most formative. It is hardly surprising that he became introspective. Some of his Etonian friends would no doubt have had a similar experience as he. Blair would not have been unique. That does not mean that he would not have been profoundly affected by his experiences.

After he left school, something very strange happened. Nothing! He did not go the Cambridge University, a step which was almost automatic for most Old Etonians, two colleges at Cambridge (Kings and Trinity) having been established in years gone by for the specific purpose of receiving these young boys and turning them into young gentlemen. Clearly, by this time, Blair was already thinking more deeply than many of his companions about the road ahead. I think it is important to take into account the year – 1903 + 18 = 1921. Blair had been eleven years of age when World War I broke out. His father may have been too old to be conscripted, but he almost certainly would be been employed at one of the War Time Ministries. Remember: this was the *first* world war. Always before, conflict had been local – two or three countries (sometimes quite small countries) were involved. It was not just that England – from across the Channel – had become involved. That had happened before. It was that England had attachments – formally known as The Empire – an important part of which (India) had been the place of Blair's birth. It was the very existence of The Empire which had made this a *world* war, which had caused the millions of deaths in Europe. Of course, England was not the only country with colonies. France, Spain, Belgium, Portugal, Holland, they all had colonies, so England *alone* was not entirely responsible for the carnage, but she, and her colonies, had been major contributors.

The young man was obviously feeling homesick. The following year (not yet quite twenty years of age) he went to Burma and joined the India Imperial Police, Burma coming under Indian control, as far as the British Empire was concerned. This Police Force was armed; the British Police Force was not. Bearing a gun while carrying out his duties did not sit well with Blair. He stayed in Burma for five years, five pivotal years. During that time, he came to hate Imperialism. On leave in England in 1927, he resigned.

Blair decided to become a writer. He made a slow start, writing short stories and novels, which nobody would print. In 1928-29, he went to live in Paris, a city which had all but been destroyed by the War. It was not just the buildings which had been damaged, but Paris' heart and soul. Blair records that he lived hand-to-mouth, going hungry several times. He lived among the poor, part-criminal element. At times he begged. At times he stole. "Their way of life interested me" (p. 115). Blair was studying different ways of living, both from the practical and the emotional perspective, the better to portray the characters in his yet-to-be-written stories. He returned to England, residing in Yorkshire, where he took the opportunity to study the conditions of work of the miners, for the same reason.

Mining was difficult and dangerous work and the miners were immensely proud of their achievements. The harder they worked, the prouder they became; the prouder they became, the harder they worked. Without them, there would be no factory furnaces producing goods, no railways, no trains. Without them, England would not have won the war. In the *Preface* to his Ukrainian edition, he wrote that he became pro-Socialist more out of disgust with the way the poorer section of the industrial workers were oppressed and neglected than out of any theoretical admiration for a planned society.

From 1934 onwards, Blair became able to support himself by the earnings from his writing.

In 1936 he married a young lady by the name of Eileen, who was to be a great help and support in all his endeavours. We know little about her, except that she did have a degree. The very week that they were married, the Spanish Civil war broke out. They went to Spain to fight for the (Socialist) Government against the Facist Interloper, Franco – although not for six months. They had to wait until Blair finished the book he was writing. They found themselves in a confused situation. Various political parties were supporting the Government. They joined the International Brigade and, more by accident than judgement, found themselves in the POUM militia – the Spanish Trotskyists, although, at that point of his life, Blair was not a committed socialist. He was not a committed anything. They had been battling for six months when Blair took a bullet which struck him in the region of the throat. Clearly, the bullet did not penetrate, because Blair survived and the photograph on the back of *Animal Farm* shows no scarring, at least above the collar and tie. Nevertheless, it was a very traumatic incident. By mid 1937, the Communists had gained the upper hand. As part of his rise to power, Stalin had replaced Trotsky. Stalin supporters considered Trotsky supporters 'the enemy'. They hunted down Trotskyists. Eric and Eileen found themselves fleeing for their lives and considered themselves fortunate to escape back to England, without further harm.

The man-hunts in Spain coincided with the purges in Russia

under Stalin. In both countries, innocent people were being thrown into prisons for suspected unorthodoxy. A decade earlier, Blair had become disillusioned by 'right-wing' Imperialism, which he considered to be too authoritative. Now he was becoming disillusioned with 'left-wing' socialism for the same reason. How easily the common people became, not merely 'influenced' by, but 'entrapped' by, totalitarian concepts, presented to them as being solely for their benefit but, in reality, being for the benefit of their rulers, who grew rich at their expense. It was not merely the 'uneducated' poorer working class people who were being deceived but the educated middle/upper classes as well – people who considered themselves democratic.

At that time, Russia was usually referred to as 'USSR' in the same way that America was referred to as 'USA'. 'USSR' stood for 'United Soviet *Socialist* Republic'. 'Socialist Republic'! Was not that the very thing Blair had hoped would replace British Imperialism? Apparently not!

Through his confusion, Blair came to an important realisation. The problem was not politics; it was human nature!

Blair had never been to Russia and had no desire to change the Russian political system. He nevertheless saw clearly how something that had seemed so right in 1917 had become so wrong by 1937. By chance, he saw a young boy driving a cart down a country lane. The cart was being drawn by a large cart horse – and cart horses were LARGE in those days. The child controlled the horse by the use of a whip – a touch here, a touch there. Had the horse wished, it could have over-turned the cart, broken free, possibly killed the boy, but certainly galloped away, a free entity. Why didn't it? Because it was behaving in the way it had been trained to behave since it was born. That was the way with all living beings, human or animal. What was the difference between them? Was there a difference between them?

And so it was that in the latter years of the 1930s, the beginnings of the book which became *Animal Farm* were conceived. The thing which separated humans from animals was knowledge, not nature. If animals learnt differently, they would behave differently – and *vice versa*.

As Spain stabilised under her new Leader, Franco, Germany stabilised under her new leader, Hitler. The years immediately following World War I had been difficult, but now Germany had entered a new era of peace and prosperity. Blair had no more idea of what was to happen than had anyone else. The novel taking shape in his mind was formed with Russia in mind, not Germany – neither the USSR nor the Germany of the 1930s having yet reached the zenith of totalitarianism. Around 1940, Blair put pen to paper, but was unable to find a publisher. Criticising Britain's staunchest ally was not seen by any publisher as being a wise move. Eventually, the book was published in 1945.

There were class divisions in Britain but there was also mutual respect between the classes, which worked in harmony for the benefit of all – or tried to. This was not the case with totalitarian regimes – not only in Russia, but also in Germany, as the world had just discovered, to its immense cost. What separated Russian socialism from British imperialism was the lack of respect its leaders had for its workers – without whose labour there would be no food, no comfortable living, no wealth. The working classes were treated like animals. What if the animals rebelled?

And so they did. Farmer Jones and his family were chased off the land. The animals had no problem bringing in the harvest. Not needing to be shared with humans, there was plenty for all. Sewing for the next season was a bit more difficult. The animals knew what to do but had difficulty doing it. Gradually they learned how to manipulate the machinery but their harvests were never as good. The pigs taught themselves to read, first from discarded children's books and then from manuals left around the farm, from which they learned how to operate the machinery. The pigs were the only ones with the intellectual capacity to learn to read. They became the rulers. They needed to learn to walk on two legs to operate equipment

– and so on. Repair items were needed. They had to be purchased. Food was traded with a nearby farmer – trade had begun. It is only a short book, one hundred pages, but every page is worth reading. The book is a perfect mix of humour and seriousness. 'Many a true word is spoken in jest' as the old saying goes. The book ends with six well-fed fat pigs sitting around one side of a table and six well-fed fat humans sitting around the other – and who could tell the difference?

The main point of the story was not the similarity of the six fat human pigs and the six fat animal pigs but the difference between the fat pigs and the rest of the animals, who did all the work.

The book was an immediate success. If some readers had Nazis in mind, rather than Stalinists, that did not matter. What mattered was the warning about how easy it was for even the best, highest-minded individuals to slip into totalitarianism. In the final stages, the pigs had become quite ruthless. They not only killed any animal proven to be of subversive mind, but any animal *suspected* of harbouring subversive thoughts – no proof required. The world was to recognise these terrible events as happening in post World War II Russia; Blair was endeavouring to draw attention to them before the war even started. The pigs (and Stalin) opined that the only means of ensuring political stability was to eliminate opposition. As stated in *Appendix 1,* 'One can only defend democracy by totalitarian methods. One must crush its enemies. The most ardent Russophile hardly believed that all of the victims were guilty of all of the things they were accused of: but by holding heretical opinions they 'objectively harmed' the regime and therefore it was quite right to massacre them' (p. 110).

Soviet society had become hierarchical, which meant that it was no longer socialist (p. 117). Blair felt that the people of England simply did not understand concentration camps, mass deportations, arrests without trial, press censorship, etc. (p. 118). He did not mention 'brain-washing', which received extensive coverage in *Nineteen Eighty-Four.*

In 1944, Eric and Eileen adopted a boy, Richard Horatio. In February 1945, Blair went to France as a War Correspondence for the *Observer*. One month later, his dearly beloved wife died unexpectedly during the course of what was expected to be a routine operation. Eric must have been devastated. One good thing did happen that year: on 17th August, 1944, *Animal Farm* was finally published. The following year, the war ended, Attlee became Prime Minister. In the *Afterword*, it is claimed that Blair whole-heartedly supported the Attlee government and its form of socialism. That may have been true in 1946 but I doubt that it was true in 1949. Blair lived long enough to witness the repetition of the pattern – from liberator to dictator, at least in its beginnings.

Had Blair's book, *Nineteen Eighty-Four*, alerted the British public to the danger? We will never know, but Attlee was voted out of office and Churchill was voted it. Blair wrote his last book after the end of the war and this time he had no problems finding a publisher. I was in my eleventh year, quite old enough to appreciate the stir it caused. We (school kids) all knew about 'Big Brother' watching us but, with no television and no security cameras, the concept of the telescreens was a bit beyond us. 'Big Brother' seemed rather like a universal Head Master, who laid down the rules. Be here by a certain time; wear certain clothes; when the bell rings, go to a certain room; take with you prescribed books; eat and drink at prescribed times and only partake of allowed foods. Walk on the left and NO running in the corridors. I resolved to wait to read the book until 1984, which I did. I have just read it for the second time and found it as abhorent second time around as I did the first. (This time, it was not the year which was '84, but me!)

It was Blair's life-long dream to live in a socialist society. He could not, because there was not one. Nevertheless, he did not live in vain. His final book made a lasting impression. Attitudes changed around the (Western) world. Every effort is still being made to oppose totalitarianism. It is an ongoing battle – but at least we are aware of the problem.

17
Full Circle

Of the people l studied during the course of this work, one stood out – Robert Owen. How appropriate, it seemed, that he had been called 'The Father of Socialism'. Still, l cannot recall hearing his name mentioned at school. l remember learning about Stevenson and the importance of steam power; l remember learning about McAdam and tarred roads; l remember learning about Arkwright and the Spinning Jenny. l just don't remember learning about Robert Owen and his cotton mill.

Whether Owen was truly wise beyond his years, waiting, listening, learning, evaluating, before acting, or whether he kept silent not to betray his ignorance, does not really matter. The result was the same. He listened and learned. The decisions he made were based upon information relevant to the situation at that time, in that place. When did it all change?

One day stands out above all others – the day of Owen's return to New Lanark – his 'Second Coming'. As a child, Owen had understood the equality of each soul, irrespective of ability or station in society. He had understood that our character was formed by our life experience, something over which a child has little, or no, control. Each persons was deserving of respect. Others had disagreed with his vision, had plotted his downfall but he had overcome. Now he was returning to reclaim his (little) kingdom, chosen, not by God, but by the people.

Was this not the essence of socialism – that the leader(s) be chosen by the people, chosen for their ability and their dedication, not by chance? The old concept that certain people were born into positions of authority, placed there by 'God' because it was His wish, was wrong. There was no 'God', only people, and it was their choice which mattered, and they had chosen him!

It was after that day that he began to invite others to visit his factory. They came, in greater and greater numbers, and not just from Britain. Any human being would have been proud. He certainly was entitled to be. But pride comes before a fall! Had Owen simply retired from New Lanark and left others (his sons) to carry on his work, how different the ending might have been. He would not have deserted his wife and daughters; he would not have squandered his family's fortune. New Lanark might have continued to be a beacon, its light spreading, by osmosis, across the land.

All was not lost. While Owen's vision of single-industry 'family' communities may not have survived, his concern for the welfare of his workers was taken up by successive governments. We take for granted legislation mandating minimum pay, overtime, meal breaks, work place health and safety, holidays, but it is to Owen's initiative that we owe all of these.

Wallace, too, understood the equality of each soul, irrespective of race, colour or place of birth. He learnt his 'lessons', not within a tiny community in a remote part of the British Isles, but by visiting other places, other islands, other communities, watching and observing how things were done, without suggesting any changes, as had done Owen. He learnt, not how to run a factory, not how to organise other peoples' lives, but of each human being's 'inalienable rights', particularly the freedom to walk the land of their birth. There was a problem here, too. That which worked well for a small community would not necessarily work well for a large one. Wallace knew of Owen's work and agreed with him that we were each the product of the society into which we had been born. He treated everyone he met with equal respect, from the Raj in his Palace to the native who slept beneath the stars. Thought, word and deed were more important than possessions.

Both men sought to lift the lower strata of society up; neither sought to bring the upper strata down. It was this lack of negativity which shone over their work and which still enlightens us today.

Owen did his best work at home. It was when he tried to spread his energies, his resources too widely, that he came to grief and I think that is a lesson we would all do well to ponder. His ego took over.

Wallace, too, did his best work at home. He was fortunate that his life's path took him overseas in his youth, where he, too, lost all that he had, but he had time to recover. Owen took to the wider world the knowledge and experience he had gained in a small community; Wallace brought back to a small country the knowledge and experience he had gained the far reaches of the world..

Ernest Haeckel combined the qualities of Owen and Wallace – in some respects. In others, he was completely different. All three rejected Christianity, the idea that God preferred one race of people above another but, whereas Owen was atheistic in his beliefs, Wallace agnostic, Haeckel had an overwhelming belief in a superior, Creative Force. So superior was this Force, that the individual person sank into insignificance. Identity lay with the group – the State. The individual might benefit from the State, but this was coincidental. Humans should emulate the ant, not the eagle. One society was not superior to another due to Divine decree. One society was superior to another due to hard work.

The bedrock of socialism was that all were born equal, irrespective of place in society. For Haeckel, all may be born equal but all did not die equal. This was true of individuals. This was true of societies. Germany had earned its place as the greatest nation on Earth as the result of its industry but would only retain that position by dint of hard work. The head said 'We are all the same'; the heart said 'No, we are not'.

Herbert Spencer could not have been more different from Wallace. He did travel – occasionally – just for a short time, but he did most of his learning sitting down, either indoors, in front of a fire, if the weather was inclement, or beneath a tree, out in the fresh air, if the weather was co-operative. His love of nature was genuine. His interest in the writing of Charles Lyell was genuine. The Universe was not the same today as it had always been; our Earth was not the same today as it had always been; societies were not the same today as they had always been. When the physical environment changed, life forms in that environment changed. Plants and animals had little, or no, control over their environment, over their development. Humans did. How people changed the society in which they lived and how that changed society changed the people was of great interest to Spencer. Of even greater interest was the number of people who read his work. There can be no doubt that Spencer wrote more to feed his ego than he did not feed the poor.

Bertrand Russell was different from the others in that he had been born into an aristocratic family. He claims that in his younger years, he rejected the concept of 'aristocracy' – was embarrassed by it – and this attitude remained with him until his brother died and the title of 'Earl' came to rest upon his shoulders.

I am sure that as a young man Bertrand genuinely believed his rejection of the superior role of the aristocracy was based on a deeply held principle, but, if that had been the case, would he not have renounced the title when he, unexpectedly, inherited it? Rather than rejecting it, he embraced it, and the longer he lived, the more he milked it for all it was worth – and it was worth plenty. Russell *thought* he was a socialist. He told people he was a socialist. He even stood for parliament as a socialist, but deep down inside he was not.

I have come to the conclusion that most of us are the same. At one level, we take upon ourselves the standards of our society. *All* young creatures are pre-programmed at birth to imitate those around them. That is how they learn. Humans, alone, have the ability, the so-called 'free will' to deviate – and look where that has got us!

And so we come to George Orwell, the most astute of them all. Orwell was a lost soul. He knew what he did not want. He did not want Imperialism. He thought he knew what he did want. He thought he wanted socialism but wherever he looked for it, he could not find it. When he left England for Burma in 1923, England was just recovering from the first World War and was experiencing the greatest change in the shortest time in its recorded history. At the beginning of the war, women still wore long skirts, long-sleeved blouses, buttoned up to the neck. All females eighteen years of age or over wore their long hair swept up. Only in the privacy of their own apartment did they ever let their hair down. By the time Eric left, less than five years after the end of the war, girls had cut their hair, shortened their skirts and become 'flappers'. They had even acquired the right to vote. How different was the country to which he returned five years later, sunk in the depths of the Deep Depression.

The country was ripe for change and no doubt Blair anticipated the establishment of a socialist society. He was to be disappointed. He tried France, Spain – worse, not better. He watched Germany and Russia, both of which countries had deposed their monarch while he was still at school. Twenty years later, what good had it done?

He, alone, of the people studied seemed to be aware of the danger posed if socialism was allowed to come 'full circle'. Like the circular rainbow, one colour blends into the next. Others had been writers: Owen, Spencer, Russell, but they had bombarded their readers with *facts*. Blair knew the value of a good story. The tale he told was was so tall that even the blind could see, so striking that even the deaf could hear and so clear that even the dumb could understand.

References

Packard, F. A. (1866) *Life of Robert Owen*. Carlisle (Mass.): Applewood Books

Podmore, F. (1906) *Robert Owen: A Biograpahy* (2 vols.). London: Hutchinson & Co.

Silver, H. (1969/2009) *Robert Owen on Education*. Cambridge: Cambridge University Press.

Orwell, G. (1949/2011)) *Nineteen Eighty-Four*. Melbourne: Penguin Group.

Owen, R. (1813/2013) *A New View of Society*. New York: Prism Key Press.

Owen, R. (1817) *Essays on the Formation of Human Character*. Palala Press.

Owen, R. (1840) *The Book of the New Moral World*. Andesite Oress.

Owen R. (1841) *Lectures on the Rational System of Society*. Sagwan Press.

Owen, R. (1849) *The Revolution in the Mind and Practice of the Human Race*. Franklin Classics.

Owen, R. (1855) *The New Existence of Man Upon the Earth*. Franklin Classics.

Owen R., Bellamy, E. and Fourier, C. (2012) *Writings of the Utopian Socialists*. St. Petersburg, Fl. Red and Black Publishers.

Owen, R. (2013) *A New View of Society*. New York: Prism Key Press.

Podmore, F. (1906) *Robert Owen: A Biography* (2 vols.) London: Hutchinson & Co.

Russell, B. (1975) *Autobiography*. London. George Allen & Unwin.

Silver, H. (1969/2009) *Robert Owen on Education*. (ed. H. Silver) Cambridge: Cambridge University Press.

Spencer, H. (1911/1919) *Essays on Education and Kindred Subjects*. London: J. M. Dent & Sons.

Spencer, H. (1882) *The Principles of Sociology: Vol.1.* New York: D. Appleton & Co.

Spencer, H. (1882) *The Principles of Sociology: Vol.2.* London: Williams and Norgate.

Spencer, H. (1912) *The Principles of Sociology: Vol.3.* New York: D. Appleton & Co.

About the Author

Denise Carrington-Smith was born in 1937. She spent her childhood in London, migrating to Australia with her young family in 1967.

Having trained in yoga, which she taught for some years, Denise qualified as a Natural Therapist, specializing in homoeopathy. She lectured in herbalism, Bach Flower Remedies and homoeopathy before establishing the Victorian College of Classical Homoeopathy, of which she was Principal for a number of years. She also served as both State and Federal President of the Australian Federation of Homoeopaths.

Recognizing the need for profressional training in counselling, Denise qualified as a psychologist and also a hypnotherapist.

Denise retired to Far North Queensland at the end of 1995, returning to University, where she took up the study of archaeology, receiving her doctorate in 2013. Denise has seven children, eighteen grandchildren and a smattering of great-grandchildren.